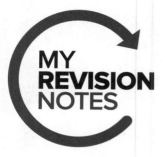

MY
REVISION
NOTES

C000125203

T-LEVELS
THE NEXT LEVEL QUALIFICATION

EDUCATION AND EARLY YEARS

Louise Burnham
Penny Tassoni

The Publishers would like to thank the following for permission to reproduce copyright material.

Photo credits

Fig 1.1 © Krakenimages.com/stock.adobe.com; Fig 1.2 © David Richards/Alamy Stock Photo; Fig 1.3 © Jacob Lund/stock.adobe.com; Fig 2.2 © Tyler Olson – Fotolia; Fig 4.5 © JulesSelmes/Hodder Education; Fig 5.1 © sturti/Getty Images; Fig 5.4 © Drobot Dean/stock.adobe.com; Fig 5.5 © Monkey Business/stock.adobe.com; Fig 6.1 l © Family Rights Group, r © Family Action 2023; Fig 6.3 © Tijana/stock.adobe.com; Fig 8.1 © Monkey Business/stock.adobe.com; Fig 8.5 © JulesSelmes/Hodder Education; Fig 9.2 © Russell Hart/Alamy Stock Photo; Fig 9.3 © Monkey Business/stock.adobe.com; Fig 10.2 © Rawpixel.com/Shutterstock.com; Fig 10.3 © Angela Hampton Picture Library/Alamy Stock Photo; Fig 11.1 © satura_/stock.adobe.com; Fig 11.3 © Paul Doyle/Alamy Stock Photo; Fig 11.4 © BSIP SA/Alamy Stock Photo; Fig 11.6 © Photographee.eu/stock.adobe.com; Fig 12.1 © DragonImages/stock.adobe.com

'T-LEVELS' is a registered trade mark of the Department for Education.

'T Level' is a registered trade mark of the Institute for Apprenticeships and Technical Education. The T Level Technical Qualification is a qualification approved and managed by the Institute for Apprenticeships and Technical Education.

Although every effort has been made to ensure that website addresses are correct at time of going to press, Hodder Education cannot be held responsible for the content of any website mentioned in this book. It is sometimes possible to find a relocated web page by typing in the address of the home page for a website in the URL window of your browser.

Hachette UK's policy is to use papers that are natural, renewable and recyclable products and made from wood grown in well-managed forests and other controlled sources. The logging and manufacturing processes are expected to conform to the environmental regulations of the country of origin.

To order, please visit www.hoddereducation.com or contact Customer Service at education@hachette.co.uk / +44 (0)1235 827827.

ISBN: 978 1 0360 0510 8

© Penny Tassoni and Louise Burnham 2023

First published in 2023 by
Hodder Education,
An Hachette UK Company
Carmelite House
50 Victoria Embankment
London EC4Y 0DZ

www.hoddereducation.com

Impression number   10 9 8 7 6 5 4 3 2 1

Year   2027 2026 2025 2024 2023

All rights reserved. Apart from any use permitted under UK copyright law, no part of this publication may be reproduced or transmitted in any form or by any means, electronic or mechanical, including photocopying and recording, or held within any information storage and retrieval system, without permission in writing from the publisher or under licence from the Copyright Licensing Agency Limited. Further details of such licences (for reprographic reproduction) may be obtained from the Copyright Licensing Agency Limited, www.cla.co.uk

Cover photo © Sergey Nivens - stock.adobe.com

Illustrations by Integra Software Services Pvt. Ltd.

Typeset by Integra Software Services Pvt. Ltd., Pondicherry, India.

Printed in Spain

A catalogue record for this title is available from the British Library.

Get the most from this book

Everyone has to decide his or her own revision strategy, but it is essential to review your work, learn it and test your understanding. These Revision Notes will help you to do that in a planned way, topic by topic. Use this book as the cornerstone of your revision and don't hesitate to write in it — personalise your notes and check your progress by ticking off each section as you revise.

Tick to track your progress

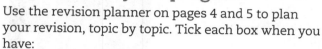

Use the revision planner on pages 4 and 5 to plan your revision, topic by topic. Tick each box when you have:

+ revised and understood a topic
+ tested yourself
+ practised the exam questions and gone online to check your answers and complete the quick quizzes.

You can also keep track of your revision by ticking off each topic heading in the book. You may find it helpful to add your own notes as you work through each topic.

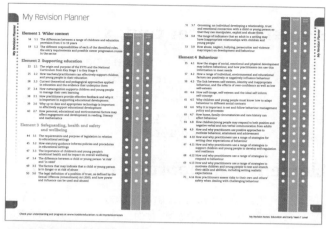

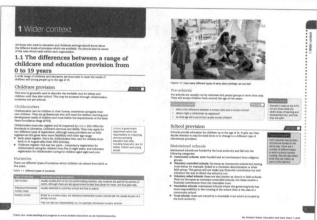

Features to help you succeed

Exam tips

Expert tips are given throughout the book to help you polish your exam technique in order to maximise your chances in the exam.

Typical mistakes

The authors identify the typical mistakes candidates make and explain how you can avoid them.

Now test yourself

These short, knowledge-based questions provide the first step in testing your learning. Answers are provided online at **www.hoddereducation.co.uk/myrevisionnotesdownloads**

Definitions and key words

Clear, concise definitions of essential key terms are provided where they first appear.

Key words from the specification are highlighted in bold throughout the book.

Making links

This feature identifies specific connections between topics and tells you how revising these will aid your exam answers.

Revision activities

These activities will help you to understand each topic in an interactive way.

Exam-style questions

Practice exam questions are provided for each topic. Use them to consolidate your revision and practise your exam skills.

Online

Go online to check your answers to the exam questions at **www.hoddereducation.co.uk/myrevisionnotesdownloads**

My Revision Notes: Education and Early Years T Level

My Revision Planner

REVISED TESTED EXAM READY

Check your understanding and progress at www.hoddereducation.co.uk/myrevisionnotes

Element 4 Behaviour

My Revision Planner

Check your understanding and progress at **www.hoddereducation.co.uk/myrevisionnotes**

REVISED   TESTED   EXAM READY

My Revision Planner

Exam practice answers online at

www.hoddereducation.co.uk/myrevisionnotesdownloads

REVISED	TESTED	EXAM READY

My Revision Planner

8

Countdown to my exams

From September

+ Attend class in person or via the internet if necessary; listen and enjoy the subject; make notes. Make friends in class and discuss the topics with them. Watch the news.

6–8 weeks to go

+ Start by looking at the specification – make sure you know exactly what material you need to revise and the style of the examination. Use the revision planner on pages 4–8 to familiarise yourself with the topics.
+ Organise your notes, making sure you have covered everything on the specification. The revision planner will help you to group your notes into topics.
+ Work out a realistic revision plan that will allow you time for relaxation. Set aside days and times for all the subjects that you need to study, and stick to your timetable.
+ Set yourself sensible targets. Break your revision down into focused sessions of around 40 minutes, divided by breaks. These Revision Notes organise the basic facts into short, memorable sections to make revising easier.

REVISED ◯

2–6 weeks to go

+ Read through the relevant sections of this book and refer to the exam tips, exam summaries, typical mistakes and key terms. Tick off the topics as you feel confident about them. Highlight those topics you find difficult and look at them again in detail.
+ Test your understanding of each topic by working through the 'Now test yourself' questions in the book. Look up the answers online at **www.hoddereducation.co.uk/myrevisionnotesdownloads**
+ Make a note of any problem areas as you revise, and ask your teacher to go over these in class.
+ Look at past papers. This is one of the best ways to revise and practise your exam skills. Write or prepare planned answers to the exam practice questions provided in this book. Check your answers online at **www.hoddereducation.co.uk/myrevisionnotesdownloads**
+ Use the revision activities to try out different revision methods. For example, you can make notes using mind maps, spider diagrams or flash cards.
+ Track your progress using the revision planner and give yourself a reward when you have achieved your target.

REVISED ◯

One week to go

+ Try to fit in at least one more timed practice of an entire past paper and seek feedback from your teacher, comparing your work closely with the mark scheme.
+ Check the revision planner to make sure you haven't missed out any topics. Brush up on any areas of difficulty by talking them over with a friend or getting help from your teacher.
+ Attend any revision classes put on by your teacher. Remember, they are an expert at preparing people for examinations.

REVISED ◯

The day before the examination

+ Flick through these Revision Notes for useful reminders, for example, the exam tips, exam summaries, typical mistakes and key terms.
+ IMPORTANT: Check the time (is it morning or afternoon?) and place of your examination. Keep in touch with other students in your class.
+ Make sure you have everything you need for the exam – pens, highlighters and water.
+ Allow some time to relax and have an early night to ensure you are fresh and alert.

REVISED ◯

My exams

Paper A

Date:...

Time: ....

Location: ....

Paper B

Date:...

Time: ....

Location: ....

Exam breakdown

To gain this qualification, you will need to pass two exams and also complete an employer set project (ESP) which assesses you in relation to the core skills but is linked to your occupational specialism (Early Years or Assisting Teaching).

This section focuses on the two exams that are linked to the core elements.

Five things you need to know about the core assessment:
1　Exams are held twice a year.
2　There are two papers – Paper A and Paper B – that cover the core elements between them.
3　Paper A covers Core elements 1–6.
4　Paper B covers Core elements 7–12.
5　Each paper is worth 35 per cent of your grade for the core component.

Question types

There are three types of question in papers A and B:
+ multiple-choice questions
+ short-answer questions
+ extended response.

You will need to be familiar with each type of question. Extended response questions are usually worth more marks than multiple-choice questions or short-answer questions.

> **Exam tips**
>
> + Always read through the whole exam paper before starting. This way you can begin to think about the extended response questions as you are doing the more straightforward questions.
> + Make sure that you leave enough time for the extended response questions. These are worth more marks than the other questions.

Multiple-choice questions

REVISED ●

Some questions in the exam will be multiple choice. These are sometimes called MCQs. To answer these, you need to select the correct answer from four options. Here is an example of a multiple-choice question:
1　A room leader works
　　a　in a day nursery
　　b　in a school
　　c　in a sixth form college
　　d　in a playgroup

How to tackle this question

Think about what a room leader does to help you identify where they work. Read through the four answers. The correct answer to this question is a.

Tips

+ Always read through all of the answers before making a decision.
+ Sometimes two answers will seem possible, but one will always be the right one in that situation.
+ If you do not know the answer, always guess. You have a one in four chance of getting it right!

Short-answer questions

Short-answer questions usually require you to write one or two sentences.

Short-answer questions are made up of command words such as 'identify' or 'describe'. Command words tell you what you need to do to answer the question. Look carefully at these before writing an answer, as the length of your answer will depend on the command.

Look at Table 0.1, produced by NCFE, which explains the meaning of different command words. These verbs are most likely to be used in a short-answer question.

Table 0.1 Command words in short-answer questions

Command word	Use
Choose	Select from a range of alternatives.
Compare	Identify similarities and/or differences.
Describe	Give an account of or set out characteristics or features.
Explain	Set out purposes or reasons or make something clear in relation to a particular situation. An explanation requires understanding to be demonstrated.
Give examples	Answers should include relevant examples in the context of the question.
Identify	Name or otherwise characterise.
List	Give a selection of answers, as many as the question indicates.
Name	Identify using a recognised technical term.
Outline	Set out main characteristics or features.
State	Express in clear, brief terms.
Summarise	Give a brief statement of the main points.

Source: NCFE T level-support materials command verbs October 2021

Revision activity

Match the command word to its correct definition:

Identify	Set out purposes or reasons or make something clear in relation to a particular situation. An explanation requires understanding to be demonstrated.
Describe	Name or otherwise characterise.
Explain	Give an account of or set out characteristics or features.

Here is an example of a short-answer question:

Identify one resource and describe how it can be used to support a child or young person with English as an additional language (EAL).

How to tackle this question

This question is in two parts.
+ First write down the name of a resource.
+ In a couple of sentences, write about what it is and how it is used.
+ For example: 'A dual language book has the text in English and the home language. It can help children and young people make the link between English words and words in their home language.'

Tips

+ Read the question carefully and underline each of the command words.
+ Look to see how many marks the question is worth. Two marks may mean that you need to put down two pieces of information.
+ Keep to the point when answering. You will not gain more marks just by writing a long answer.

Typical mistake

Remember not to write more information than is needed in a short-answer question. If you do, you will not have enough time to complete the extended response questions.

Extended response

Paper A and Paper B will each have a small number of questions that require a longer answer, and more marks are available for these questions.

Extended response questions usually require you to show that you are able to analyse information and also apply knowledge to a situation. You may include an example to make your point. For example: 'While reward charts may work in the short term, additional strategies *such as involving a child in their learning* may provide longer-term motivation.'

Read the command words carefully, and make sure that your answers meet the requirements of the question.

Look at Table 0.2, produced by NCFE. It explains the meaning of different command words that might be used in an extended response question.

Table 0.2 Command words in extended response questions

Command word	Use
Assess	Evaluate or estimate the quality of a given topic to make an informed judgement; may include advantages and disadvantages.
Analyse	Separate information into component parts. Make logical, evidence-based connections between the components.
Consider	Review and respond to given information.
Describe	Give an account of or set out characteristics or features.
Discuss	Present key points about different ideas or strengths and weaknesses of an idea. There should be some element of balance, although not necessarily equal weighting.
Evaluate	Review information and bring it together to make judgements and conclusions from available evidence. Students may also use their own understanding to consider evidence for and against.
Explain	Set out purposes or reasons or make something clear in relation to a particular situation. An explanation requires understanding to be demonstrated.
Justify	Support a case or idea with evidence. This might reasonably involve discussing and discounting alternative views or actions.
Show	Provide structured evidence to reach a conclusion.
Summarise	Brief statement of the main points.
Suggest (what/why/how)	Present a possible cause or solution. Apply knowledge to a new situation to provide a reasoned explanation.
Use or using	Answer must be based on information given in the question. In some cases, students may be asked to use their own knowledge and understanding.

Source: NCFE T level-support materials command verbs October 2021

Note that the command words 'describe' and 'explain' may be used in both short-answer and extended response questions.

Revision activity	
Match each word to the correct definition:	
Discuss	Review information and bring it together to make judgements and conclusions from available evidence. Students may also use their own understanding to consider evidence for and against.
Evaluate	Support a case or idea with evidence. This might reasonably involve discussing and discounting alternative views or actions.
Justify	Present key points about different ideas or strengths and weaknesses of an idea. There should be some element of balance, although not necessarily equal weighting.

Check your understanding and progress at **www.hoddereducation.co.uk/myrevisionnotes**

Tips

+ Underline the command words when looking at an extended response question.
+ Read through your answer and check for punctuation and spellings. For these higher-level questions, extra marks are available for 'quality of written communication'.

Here is an example of an extended answer question:

Evaluate **three** strategies to support children and young people to develop self-regulation.

How to tackle this question

+ First, you need to choose three strategies.
+ For each strategy, explain how it could support self-regulation.
+ Write about the advantages and disadvantages of the strategies. For example, do any have drawbacks, or are not suitable in some situations? What are the advantages of using one strategy as compared to another?

> **Typical mistake**
>
> Don't only describe or explain a strategy. If you forget to evaluate its effectiveness, you will lose marks.

Some extended response questions require quite long responses. The question may be in several parts. Make sure you have addressed each part of the question in your answer. Sometimes case studies are used for these types of questions.

Here is an example:

Marcus is two years and six months old. He lives with his mother and father. He attends nursery three days a week. At his two-year progress check, his expressive language has been raised as a concern. He points to objects but can say fewer than five words.

+ Explain the importance of assessment in the early years.
+ Identify two strategies that might support Marcus' language development.
+ Consider the value of working in partnership with Marcus' parents.

How to tackle this question

Start by looking carefully at the age of the child. In this case Marcus is only two years old. Your answer must reflect this.

The question is divided into three parts. Write your answer in three parts.

1 Give reasons why assessment is important and link this to Marcus' situation. For example, what might have happened if Marcus' language delay had not been noticed?
2 There are many strategies that support language development, but you need to choose two that are relevant for his age group.
3 With examples, write about the benefits for Marcus if the setting and the parents work together. Include examples of how this might work in practice while showing how they will benefit Marcus. For example, Marcus' parents may provide information about his interests at home that can be used to plan activities that will encourage him to participate.

You will need to make more than one point to show a depth of understanding and knowledge.

> **Typical mistake**
>
> Remember:
> + to provide answers that are relevant to the information given in the case study
> + not to include more information than is required. If the question asks for two strategies, do not include three!

All those who work in education and childcare settings should know about the different kinds of provision which are available. You should also be aware of the roles which exist within each organisation.

1.1 The differences between a range of childcare and education provision from 0 to 19 years

A wide range of childcare and education services exist to meet the needs of children and young people up to the age of 19.

Childcare provision

REVISED ⬤

This term is generally used to describe the available care for babies and children until they start school. This may be accessed through childminders, nurseries and pre-schools.

Childminders

Childminders care for children in their homes, sometimes alongside their own children. They are professionals who will meet the welfare, learning and development needs of children and must follow the requirements of the Early Years Foundation Stage (EYFS).

Childminders must also register and be inspected by Ofsted (the Office for Standards in Education, Children's Services and Skills). They may apply for two different types of registration, although many providers are on both registers as this gives them more flexibility with their age range:

+ Early years register: this is for childminders who care for children from birth to 31 August after their fifth birthday.
+ Childcare register: this has two parts – compulsory registration for childminders caring for children from five to eight years, and voluntary registration for childminders caring for children aged eight and over.

> **Ofsted** A government department which has responsibility for inspecting services providing education and skills, including those who care for babies, children and young people.

Nurseries

There are different types of nurseries which children can attend from birth to five years.

Table 1.1 Different types of nurseries

Type of nursery	Explanation and description
Day nursery	Usually private and run by non-profit-making charities, day nurseries are paid for by parents or carers, although there are also government-funded free places for three- and four-year-olds.
Statutory/maintained nursery class	Usually attached to a primary school and free to attend.
Nursery school	Similar to a nursery class, but statutory/maintained nursery schools will not usually be part of a primary school. They can also be independently run, for example, Montessori nursery schools.

Figure 1.1 How many different types of early years settings can you list?

Pre-schools

Pre-schools are usually run by volunteer-led parent groups in term time only. They will accept children from around the age of two years.

Now test yourself	TESTED ◯

1 What is the difference between a nursery class and a nursery school?
2 Where might a childminder be registered?
3 At what age will a pre-school usually accept children?

Making links

Element 2 looks at the EYFS. Do you know what the seven areas of learning and development are, and how they are split?

School provision

REVISED ◯

Schools provide education for children up to the age of 16. Pupils can then decide whether to stay for sixth form or to change to a different type of educational provision.

Maintained schools

Maintained schools are funded by the local authority and fall into the following categories:

+ **Community schools**: state-funded and no involvement from religious groups.
+ **Voluntary controlled schools**: the same as community schools but having trust status, for example, linked to a Christian denomination or other faith group. This group will not make any financial contribution but will influence the way in which the school is run.
+ **Voluntary aided schools**: these are also known as church or faith schools. They are the same as voluntary controlled schools, but these receive a financial contribution from the charitable trust.
+ **Foundation schools**: maintained schools where the governing body has more responsibility in the running of the school than is the case at a community school.
+ **Trust schools**: these are owned by a charitable trust which is funded by the local authority.

Typical mistake

Don't assume that all state schools are funded in the same way. There are a number of different ways in which schools receive funding. This will also affect what they are called, as seen in this element.

+ **Special schools**: these are designed to meet the education and health needs of some children and young people with Special Educational Needs and Disability (SEND; see Element 11). The local authority may run the school or pay for places if the school is run privately or by a charitable trust.

Non-maintained schools

+ **Academies and Free schools**: these schools receive funding directly from central government through the Education Funding Agency and are run by a charitable trust.

Academies may also work with others in the area, and this may be called a Multi Academy Trust (MAT). They do not have to follow the National Curriculum and have more freedom in what they teach, although they must still carry out assessments.

The difference between academies and Free schools is that Free schools are newly formed schools, but academies have converted from being state schools which were maintained by the local authority.

+ **Private schools**: these are also known as independent schools. They receive no government funding and are paid for by fees. They may also have charitable status in exchange for offering some free scholarship places. They do not have to follow the National Curriculum.

Revision activity

Create a table: make a list of the different types of maintained schools, and highlight what they have in common and their differences.

Post-16 provision

REVISED ●

School sixth forms

Sixth forms are made up of Year 12 and 13 students and are based in schools. They usually offer A levels, International Baccalaureate or technical qualifications at Level 3.

General further education and tertiary colleges

Further education (FE) colleges and tertiary colleges usually offer a wider range of provision through the different levels of qualifications which are offered. For example, they may offer courses starting at Level 1 qualifications and can go up to Level 5.

They may also specialise in subjects such as art, drama, music or agriculture.

Private, independent and voluntary providers

These may offer training or study programmes linked to employment, for example, through apprenticeships.

Employers

After the age of 16, young people may seek employment-based training or apprenticeships which enable them to combine study with a placement provided by an employer.

Sixth form colleges

These will be specifically for 16–18-year-olds. Sixth form colleges are usually larger than the sixth forms in schools, and offer a wider range of courses.

Special colleges/specialist colleges

Special colleges may be residential and are focused on the needs of young people with special educational needs and disabilities (SEND).

These should not be confused with specialist colleges, which usually focus on a particular specialist subject area such as agriculture and horticulture.

Further education colleges These include general FE and tertiary colleges, sixth form colleges and specialist colleges, as well as adult education provision.

Tertiary colleges Institutions which provide general and vocational FE for students aged 16–19. They are distinct from general FE colleges as they cater for a specific age group and offer a less extensive and varied curriculum.

Check your understanding and progress at **www.hoddereducation.co.uk/myrevisionnotes**

Art, design and performing arts colleges

These colleges enable students to develop the skills to specialise in the arts and work in different roles in this sector.

Figure 1.2 Can you think of all the places where 16–18-year-olds might go for further study after GCSEs or other Level 2 qualifications?

Higher education institutions

Higher education institutions (HEIs) such as universities offer undergraduate and postgraduate programmes of study, which can be taken following A levels or other Level 3 qualifications.

Making links

Element 2 also looks at post-16 options for children and young people. What qualifications would be appropriate for a student who would prefer to follow a vocational route after GCSEs?

Now test yourself TESTED

4 What is the difference between a maintained and non-maintained school?

5 Name two features of a private or independent school.

6 In what form do private, independent and voluntary providers support education and training post-16?

7 How might a sixth form college differ from a school sixth form?

8 What is an HEI?

Exam-style question

1 Which one of the following statements best describes how a maintained school is funded?

A by a religious group

B by a charitable trust

C by the local authority

D directly from central government

[1]

How and when education became compulsory in England, including how this has changed over time

REVISED

In England, education has changed since becoming a legal requirement in 1870, particularly in terms of start and end dates for schooling.

Table 1.2 Changes in the law for education

Year	Change/law	What this meant for children and young people
1870	Elementary Education Act 1870	Provision of education is introduced for children aged 5–13, and is compulsory from 5 to 10 years until attainment of the 'educational standard'.
1893	School leaving age raised to 11	
1899	School leaving age raised to 12	
1921	School leaving age raised to 14	
1944	Education Act 1944	Education is free and compulsory for all children within primary and secondary schools between the ages of 5 and 15.
1972	School leaving age raised to 16	
1988	Education Reform Act 1988	Compulsory National Curriculum introduced. Standardised assessment at ages 7, 11, 14 and 16.
2008	Education and Skills Act 2008	16–18-year-olds in England must stay in education or training.

Why education is regulated

REVISED

Regulation is necessary to ensure consistency and maintain standards in the way in which education is delivered.

> **Regulation** A set of rules or laws to control and protect the way in which something is done.

Department for Education (DfE)

A government department responsible for children's services and education, in particular teaching and learning. The DfE also produces key publications including statutory guidance to support legislation.

Office for Standards in Education, Children's Services and Skills (Ofsted)

The regulator and inspector of safeguarding, education and skills settings for learners of all ages from babies upwards.

Office of Qualifications and Examinations Regulation (Ofqual)

The regulator of qualifications, assessments and examinations in England. All new qualifications must be checked and approved by Ofqual to ensure that they meet an appropriate standard.

Now test yourself

TESTED

9 When did education become free and compulsory in England for children aged 5–15, and what was the name of the Act?

10 When was the National Curriculum introduced, and which Act/legislation introduced it?

11 What is the DfE and what is it responsible for?

12 Describe the main role of Ofqual.

1.2 The different responsibilities of each of the identified roles, the entry requirements and possible career progression routes in the sector

General roles

REVISED ⬤

Table 1.3 Different responsibilities, entry requirements and possible career progression routes for each identified role

Title	Role and responsibilities	Entry requirements/progression
Early years practitioner (EYP)	Level 2 qualified early years professional: ✛ works with others to meet babies' and children's individual care needs ✛ works with others to plan, observe and report on children's learning and development ✛ promotes effective interactions.	No previous experience or qualifications needed prior to this role, although a job or volunteer placement is needed to complete the course. Progression to Level 3 early years educator qualification.
Early years educator (EYE)	Level 3 qualified early years professional. All EYP responsibilities as above and in addition: ✛ may have a managerial or other leadership role ✛ key person ✛ observing and planning next steps for learning ✛ meeting the requirements of the EYFS Statutory Framework.	No previous experience but Level 2 maths and English is usually required to work at this level and gain licence to practise. Progression can be to different job roles including nursery practitioner, assistant in Reception classes or pre-school worker. Further qualifications may include foundation degree in early years or Level 4 Certificate for the Early Years Advanced Practitioner.
Room leader	Experienced EYE responsible for the running of a room, such as a baby room or a pre-school room. Responsibilities as above. In addition they may be responsible for peer observations, appraisals and other performance management.	Room leaders need a Level 3 qualification and relevant experience. Could progress to higher management, Early Years foundation degree or other pathways such as childminding.
Teaching assistant (TA)	Supporting teaching and learning for individual pupils or small groups, working alongside teachers in primary or secondary schools. May also work one-to-one with a pupil with SEND.	TAs can start with little or no experience, although some is usually preferred. Qualifications range from Level 1 to Level 4. HLTA status (higher-level teaching assistant – remember that this is not a qualification) is also available through schools for existing assistants working at this level, enabling them to have more responsibility. TAs can progress to teacher training qualifications or foundation degrees.
Teacher/lecturer	Responsible for planning, teaching and developing the skills of children and adults in schools and colleges, as well as monitoring progress.	A degree and qualified teacher status (QTS) is required for school-based teachers. Lecturers are likely to need industry or other workplace experience, as well as a teaching qualification such as PTLLS (Preparing to Teach in the Lifelong Learning Sector) or the Level 3 award in Education and Training (RQF). Progression can include management or specialist roles in their chosen sector. ➜

Title	Role and responsibilities	Entry requirements/progression
Head teacher	Responsible for the day-to-day running of a school, as well as: + managing staff, including recruitment, meetings, training, appraisals and disciplinary procedures + working closely with the governing body and in partnership with parents + monitoring teaching and learning.	Head teachers usually have teaching experience, and have often spent time in a senior leadership role within a school. They may progress to managing an MAT or working in an advisory role.

Now test yourself TESTED ○

13 What are two of the responsibilities of an early years practitioner?

14 What qualifications and training might a teaching assistant have?

15 How might a teacher progress further?

16 Name three duties of a room leader.

17 How might a head teacher progress to another role?

Specialist roles

REVISED ○

In most of these specialist roles, the individual will also have a teaching or other responsibility within the setting, and in some cases will also be a senior manager.

Table 1.4 Specialist roles

Title	Role and responsibilities	Entry requirements/progression
Special educational needs and disabilities co-ordinator (SENDCo)	All schools and early years settings will have a SENDCo. FE colleges will need to have a designated person for students with SEND. Responsible for ensuring the best possible outcomes for children and young people with SEND. They work with parents, staff and professionals from outside agencies to achieve this.	QTS and National Award for SEN Co-ordination. A SENDCo may progress to a more senior management role within an educational setting.
Designated Safeguarding Lead (DSL)	Also known as the Designated Safeguarding Officer (DSO). Responsible for safeguarding within the school or early years setting. All staff must know who they are and that they must report concerns to them.	Usually a member of the senior management team in a school, specifically the SENDCo or head teacher. This is an additional management responsibility so there is no specific progression.
Designated person	Responsible for a specified area, for example, safeguarding or special educational needs as above. They will have other responsibilities such as a teaching or management role. Staff will need to be aware of their role so that they can request help or advice.	This is an additional management responsibility so there is no specific progression.
Mental health lead	Responsible for mental health within the school or early years setting. They will have other responsibilities such as a teaching or management role. Staff will need to be aware of their identity so that they can request help or advice.	Usually an existing member of staff who has been trained for this role. This is an additional staff responsibility so there is no specific progression.
Mentor/pastoral support	Responsible for students' pastoral care and emotional wellbeing. Learning mentors and those offering pastoral support help children and young people to overcome a range of social and emotional issues.	Mentors are usually experienced members of staff who may also have additional training. This is an additional staff responsibility so there is no specific progression.
Physical activity and nutrition co-ordinator (PANCo)	A new role in early years settings – responsible for promoting physical activity and nutrition. A PANCo will achieve this through advising staff and liaising with parents.	Specific training and certification at Level 4. This is an additional staff responsibility so there is no specific progression. →

Check your understanding and progress at **www.hoddereducation.co.uk/myrevisionnotes**

Title	Role and responsibilities	Entry requirements/progression
Counsellor	To support and guide students with a range of issues and to refer them to specialist outside agencies where appropriate. In England, provision of counsellors is not currently government-funded.	BACP (British Association for Counselling and Psychotherapy) training is needed to be a counsellor in a school or college setting. There is no specific progression route.
Careers advisor	To advise students about a range of training, qualifications and careers.	A careers advisor may have worked in a range of settings or have experience of different roles. There is no specific progression.

Figure 1.3 Who might a SENDCo need to work with in a school or early years setting?

Now test yourself TESTED ⚪

18 What are the entry requirements for being a SENDCo?

19 What support is offered by a mentor/pastoral support ?

20 What is the role of a PANCo and where would they be based?

21 What training is required to be a school counsellor?

22 What is meant by a designated person?

Exam-style question

2 Fran is a teaching assistant working in a primary school setting. She is qualified at Level 2 and has been employed to work with a named pupil in Year 3 who has SEND. Fran would like to progress in her role and is considering a range of options that will enable her to train as a teacher in the future.

Describe the different paths that Fran could take to achieve her ambition, and evaluate the advantages and disadvantages of each. [4]

2 Supporting education

There are many aspects involved in supporting children and young people with their education. This element covers a wide range of topics and you will require more revision time for this than some other elements.

2.1 The origin and purpose of the EYFS and the National Curriculum from Key Stage 1 to Key Stage 4

You need to know about each of the following stages of education in England:
+ EYFS: 0 to 5, covering the Early Years Foundation Stage
+ primary education: 5 to 11, covering Key Stages (KS) 1 and 2
+ secondary education: 11 to 16, covering KS3 and KS4
+ post-16 education: 16 to 19 (academic and technical)

EYFS

REVISED ◯

Five things to know about the EYFS statutory framework:
1 The purpose of the EYFS is to ensure that early years settings meet certain standards of education and care.
2 It is statutory, meaning that all early years settings and Reception classes have to follow it.
3 It covers the age range 0–5 years.
4 There are two main sections:
   + learning and development requirements
   + safeguarding and welfare requirements.
5 Ofsted inspects how well early years settings and Reception classes are delivering the EYFS.

> **EYFS** Early Years Foundation Stage.
>
> **Statutory** Something that is required by law.

> **Making links**
>
> Look at Element 1, Section 1.1 on page 14. Write down two different types of early years setting. Are you familiar with them?

Learning and development requirements in the EYFS

There are seven areas of learning and development. These are split into prime areas and specific areas.

There are three prime areas of development:
+ personal, social and emotional development
+ communication and language development
+ physical development.

These are seen as essential for later learning and development. They are the focus for work with babies and toddlers.

There are four specific areas of development:
+ literacy
+ mathematics
+ understanding the world (starting points for later teaching of history, geography and science)
+ expressive arts and design (starting points for art, dance and drama).

Each area of learning and development has learning outcomes, called the Early Learning Goals. Children who have met the early learning goals at the end of Reception will be ready for formal teaching in Year 1.

> **Early Learning Goals** Age-appropriate expectations in each area of development at the end of the EYFS.

Check your understanding and progress at **www.hoddereducation.co.uk/myrevisionnotes**

Now test yourself

TESTED ◯

1   Give an example of a prime area in the EYFS.
2   What is meant by the term 'Early Learning Goal'?

Assessment in the early years

There are three points at which children will be assessed in their early years.

Table 2.1 Assessment in the early years

Assessment	When	Why	Purpose
Progress check at age two	After children turn two	Required by EYFS framework	✚ Checks how children are doing in prime areas. ✚ Identifies whether children may need additional support.
Reception Baseline Assessment (RBA)	Within six weeks of a child starting Reception class	Required by DfE	✚ Provides information about children's starting points in communication and language, literacy and mathematics. ✚ Information is used to assess how well schools are supporting children to make progress during the primary years.
Foundation Stage profile	Towards end of the Reception year	Required by the EYFS framework	✚ Assessment of the early learning goals in each area of learning and development.

Typical mistake

Remember that RBA is not a requirement of the EYFS framework. It is a separate assessment required by the DfE.

Exam tip

Remember that only the prime areas are assessed for the progress check at age two.

Primary and secondary education

REVISED ◯

Here are three key things that you need to learn about primary and secondary education for this qualification:

1   how it is organised
2   the structure of the curriculum and who has to follow it
3   subjects that are included at different ages.

Organisation of primary and secondary education

School-age education is divided into key stages.

Table 2.2 The key stages of school-age education

School	Key stage	Age group
Primary	KS1	5–7 years
	KS2	7–11 years
Secondary	KS3	11–14 years
	KS4	14–16 years

The National Curriculum

Since 1988 there has been a National Curriculum in England, which it is compulsory for local authority-funded schools to follow. Its purpose is to make sure that all pupils receive a similar level of education.

The National Curriculum outlines what needs to be taught in each key stage. It was recently decided that schools funded directly by the DfE, such as academies, can opt out of teaching the National Curriculum, but if they do, they must show that their curriculum is at least equivalent to the standards of the National Curriculum.

The National Curriculum has core and foundation subjects.

Making links

Read about the types of school in Element 1. Which types of schools do not need to follow the National Curriculum?

23

Core subjects are seen as essential and are required for all key stages. They are:

+ English
+ mathematics
+ science.

The foundation subjects are shown in Figure 2.1.

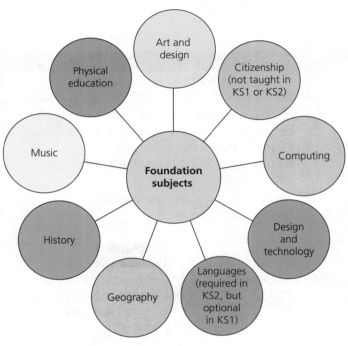

Figure 2.1 Foundation subjects

At KS4, citizenship, computing and physical education remain compulsory. Other foundation subjects become optional but may be studied as GCSEs.

At the end of KS4, young people may decide to take Level 2 qualifications such as GCSEs or a variety of technical qualifications.

There are other requirements for schools:
+ State schools have to hold collective worship, which usually takes place as part of an assembly.
+ Relationship and health education is required in all key stages.
+ Sex education is required in KS3 and KS4.

Post-16 education: 16 to 19 (A levels and technical)

REVISED

There are several education options for young people aged 16 to 19 years:
+ A levels: academic qualifications that may be used to study a subject further at university.
+ Level 3 technical qualifications such as T levels: these are delivered in HE or sixth form colleges, often involving an industry placement. This gives the option of going straight into employment or going to university.
+ Apprenticeships: a qualification is gained while working, with assessors visiting the apprentice and checking their competency.

If a young person has not gained a GCSE or other Level 2 qualification in maths or English, they must continue to study these subjects until they have passed.

Now test yourself

TESTED

3 Would a 15-year-old be required to study a language?
4 What is the difference between an apprenticeship and a technical qualification?
5 What are the three core subjects of the National Curriculum?

Check your understanding and progress at **www.hoddereducation.co.uk/myrevisionnotes**

Exam-style questions

1 Yasmin is nearly 16 years old. Her school sent her on work experience to a firm of solicitors, as she is very interested in becoming a lawyer. Yasmin has done some research and realises that the quickest route to become qualified is to take a university degree. She is taking eight GCSEs and a technical qualification at Level 2.

What type of course would suit her best following her GCSEs? [4]

2 Which of these is a prime area of learning and development within the EYFS?

A understanding the world

B mathematics

C communication

D physical development [1]

3 Which of these types of schools is required to follow the National Curriculum?

A Free school

B independent school

C local authority-funded

D academy [1]

4 Is a childminder required to follow the EYFS? [1]

2.2 How teachers/practitioners can effectively support children and young people in their education

The way that teachers and practitioners act makes a significant difference. This qualification specification lists seven ways to effectively support children and young people. For each one, you should know why it is important and be ready to give an example of each.

Table 2.3 Ways of supporting children and young people during their education

Way of supporting	Why it is important	Example
Involving children and young people in planning their own learning	Helps motivation and concentration.	+ Giving children and young people a choice of activity. + Giving a child or young person a choice of revision activities.
Communicating clearly, using positive and appropriate language for age and stage of development	Makes understanding and remembering information easier. If the language level is not right for the child or young person, they will not understand and may not learn. If the tone is negative, children and young people may respond negatively.	+ Gaining attention and making eye contact. + If needed, simplifying sentences and explaining what words mean.
Giving effective feedback and facilitating children's and young people's self-assessment	Helps children and young people know what they are doing well and understand how they can improve specific skills or knowledge.	+ Asking a young person what they feel they have done well, and identifying a specific area for improvement.
Managing own and others' time	Makes lessons and sessions run smoothly and so increases learning time.	+ Starting lessons and sessions on time. + Preparing the resources and activities ahead. + Helping children and young people to use their time effectively.
Providing nurturing experiences and opportunities to support children and young people to be able to express feelings	A nurturing environment helps promote positive behaviour. Helping children and young people to express their feelings means that they are more likely to cope with set backs.	Giving children and young people opportunities to talk about how they are feeling. + Creating a calm environment. + Praising children and young people when they talk about or cope with strong emotions. →

Way of supporting	Why it is important	Example
Observing and assessing individuals, providing tailored interventions through early identification	Ensures that children or young people who need additional support are recognised. Can identify where a strategy for teaching a topic is not working, e.g. several children/young people have not understood a concept.	✦ Hearing a child or young person read and checking that the text has been understood. ✦ Class test on a topic that has recently been taught.
Engaging **disengaged** children/young people by involving them in their own learning and assessment	Prevents the gap in knowledge and skills between them and engaged children becoming wider. Can help children and young people to become more motivated.	✦ Asking a child or young person about the conditions or resources that help them to learn best. ✦ Taking time to provide individual feedback.

Disengaged Where a child or young person is not motivated to learn.

Making links

✦ Managing behaviour links to Element 4. List three ways in which adults may support positive behaviour.

✦ Observing and assessing individuals links to Element 8. Why is assessment important when working with children and young people?

Figure 2.2 Identify two ways in which this adult might be supporting this child's learning

Now test yourself   TESTED ◯

6   Explain why giving effective feedback can support children's and young people's learning.

7   What is the link between communication and learning?

8   Give an example of involving children in their own planning.

Revision activity

Draw a spider diagram with 'Ways of supporting children/young people' in the centre and write a way of supporting education on each leg.

See how many of the seven ways you can remember. Then check your answers and add those you missed

Understand the attributes that inform professional behaviour and why they are important to effectively support education

REVISED ◯

Professional behaviour is about the personal attributes needed to work effectively with children and young people. Ten attributes for professional behaviour are given in the specification. You will need to know why they are important and how they can be seen in practice.

Check your understanding and progress at **www.hoddereducation.co.uk/myrevisionnotes**

Table 2.4 Ten attributes for professional behaviour

Attribute	Why it is important	Example of good practice
Approachability	If a child or young person has a problem or does not understand something, they are more likely to seek out help.	Greeting children and young people warmly. Good communication skills.
Confidence	Makes children and young people feel that they can trust the adult to keep them safe.	Clear communication. Being ready to challenge unwanted behaviour.
Empathy	If the adult recognises how a child or young person might be feeling, they can meet their needs more effectively.	Observing body language and carefully listening to understand what a child or young person might be feeling.
Knowledge	Required so that the teacher/practitioner can teach skills and concepts effectively.	Learning the names of types of tree before going on a nature walk.
Passion	Needed to inspire and motivate children and young people to learn.	Enthusiastic response to children's and young people's attempts or suggestions.
Patience	Needed to cope with setbacks or when a child or young person needs more time or support to learn a skill, knowledge or concept.	Taking time to explain something again, or waiting for everyone to finish.
Positivity	Being positive in a range of situations can motivate children and young people, and also help them shape their own responses to difficult situations.	Showing enthusiasm. Responding positively when there are changes or difficulties.
Reflection	Helps to improve practice or meet a child's or young person's individual needs.	Thinking about why an activity did not hold a group's interest.
Resourcefulness	Required in order to respond to unexpected situations, or to adapt teaching style and resources to meet individual needs.	Adapting a resource to make it easier.
Respect for others	Helps to build relationships with children and young people which can help with motivation and behaviour. Needed in order to build trust and work effectively with other adults, including parents.	Listening to others' ideas, suggestions and points of view. Being polite and thoughtful.

Now test yourself TESTED

9   Give an example of the impact on a child or young person if a teacher/practitioner were not approachable.

10 Explain how respect for others is an important attribute for education and childcare professionals.

11 Give an example of how a lack of patience on the part of an adult might negatively impact on learning.

Revision activity

You might find it helpful to remember the attributes by focusing on their initial letters. Using the prompts below, write out as many attributes as you can that begin with these initial letters:

✚ ACE+K

✚ PPP

✚ RRR

Exam-style question

5   Harry is 12 years old, finds most lessons boring and is falling behind in most subjects apart from mathematics. His head of year is trying to find out why Harry is doing well in this subject but not in others.

Harry says that Mr Dyson makes things interesting. Harry feels that he can always ask him a question or put his hand up for help. He says that Mr Dyson always has time for him and that if he gets an answer wrong, he is not made to feel stupid. Instead, Mr Dyson has a way of making any mistake feel like something to learn from.

Discuss the potential impact of teachers' and practitioners' professional behaviour on children's and young people's learning and development. [6]

27

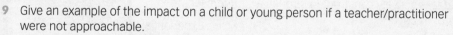

2.3 Current theoretical and pedagogical approaches applied in education and the evidence that underpins them

How schools and early years settings approach teaching and learning is often influenced by one or more theoretical approaches. You need to show that you understand the features of and evidence to support each of the approaches as well as the theorists that are associated with them.

> **Exam tips**
>
> ✚ When planning your revision, make sure that you allow sufficient time to learn this section very thoroughly. A question about theoretical approaches is very likely to appear.
> ✚ Remember also that in this specification, some theorists are linked to more than one approach.

It is a good idea to revise this section in three stages.

Start your revision by learning the information in this table.

Table 2.5 Current theoretical and pedagogical approaches

	Approach	Key features	Underpinning evidence/Advocates of this approach
1	Behaviourism	Learning is a result of external stimuli rather than cognitive processes. Consequences of responses can strengthen or lessen. Teachers are more likely to direct instruction.	Pavlov's Dogs study Watson's Little Albert Experiment Skinner's study of operant conditioning (Skinner box) The Education Endowment Foundation's review of Ark Mathematics Mastery Project
2	Cognitive constructivism	Learning builds on what students already know and can do. Knowledge is actively constructed through a process of discovery. Learning follows a sequence of stages.	Piaget's Four Stages of Development Jerome Bruner's Three Models of Representation Kolb's Experiential Learning Cycle Bloom's Taxonomy
3	Social constructivism	Learning is an active social process between teachers and peers. Students' understanding and knowledge of the world is based on the quality of interactions with others. The learning environment, home environment, culture and society can influence the quality of interactions.	Bergmann and Sams' *Flip Your Classroom* Bruner's Discovery Learning Marion Dowling's *Young Children's Thinking* Cathy Nutbrown's *Threads of Thinking* *The 30 Million Word Gap* by Hart and Risley Vygotsky's Zone of Proximal Development
4	Connectivism	Technology has created new ways for people to share knowledge and learn from others. Learners can shape their own learning in a variety of ways, e.g. by visiting websites, messaging others and being part of an online community.	Downes' Modernised learning delivery strategies Siemens' 'A Learning theory for the digital age' and 'Massive open online courses: Innovation in education?' Lave and Wenger's community of practice →

Check your understanding and progress at **www.hoddereducation.co.uk/myrevisionnotes**

	Approach	Key features	Underpinning evidence/Advocates of this approach
5	Humanism	Individuals construct knowledge in the context of their own unique feelings, values and experiences. Feelings are as important as knowledge in the learning process. The teacher's role is to facilitate rather than deliver learning. Learning should be personalised to each individual student. A student's person potential can only be fulfilled when their physical and affective needs have been met. Humans are intentional and seek meaning, value and creativity.	Malaguzzi's '100 languages of a child' (Reggio Emilia approach) Paulo Freire's *Pedagogy of the oppressed* Bronfenbrenner's ecological system United Nations Convention on the Rights of the Child 1989 Maslow's hierarchy of needs Carl Rogers' *Freedom to Learn*

Now test yourself TESTED ⬤

12 Which approach involves learners mainly using technology for learning?

13 Bruner's three models of representation is an example of which pedagogical approach?

14 Which approach considers social interactions important in learning?

Revision activity

Create a simple table with two columns.
+ Write down the five theoretical approaches in one column.
+ Next to each theoretical approach, write down at least two advocates of this approach.

Behaviourism

REVISED ⬤

Behaviourism is an approach that is often used to shape children and young people's behaviour. It can also be used as a way of helping children and young people remember information. An example of behaviourism is when children learn their multiplication tables by rote in order to get praise or reward.

The term 'conditioning' is an important feature in behaviourism. It refers to the way that responses are shaped as a result of what happens to the child or young person. The term 'stimuli' is used to describe the 'triggers' or the 'what happens' part of the process.

There are two types of conditioning.

Classical conditioning

This occurs when the stimuli is presented first, for example, a bell rings before a dog is fed. After a while the dog learns that the bell signals food and becomes excited.

Two experiments showed how classical conditioning worked.
1 Ivan Pavlov did a study showing that dogs could be trained to salivate if they heard a bell, even when eventually no food was given.
2 John Watson showed that classical conditioning could create a phobia in a child. The child, named as 'Little Albert', became afraid of a rat because a loud noise was made each time he saw the rat.

Operant conditioning

Operant conditioning uses **reinforcers**, including rewards, after the stimuli to strengthen or weaken the responses. For example, a child keeps working hard because they want a sticker from the teacher. The sticker is a reinforcer.

29

The use of rewards (positive reinforcement) to modify behaviour was a particular feature of B.F. Skinner's behaviourist approach. He used the term **operant conditioning** to describe how positive and negative reinforcements could shape learning including behaviour. Stickers, praise and sanctions are examples of how his theory is used in practice.

> **Sanction** The stated consequence for a child or young person of showing unwanted behaviour.

There are two important things to remember about behaviourism:
+ **Continuity:** Behaviourism can be used to support learning and shape behaviour BUT information may not be retained if it is not practised for a while.
+ **Motivation:** The learner is motivated by the reinforcement, such as getting a sticker or praise from the teacher. If positive reinforcement stops, learners may not continue with the activity.

Behaviourism is therefore rarely used as a single approach when teaching. This is because it is thought that when a child or young person is motivated by a desire to learn something, retention and understanding of information is better.

Key points to remember

The chart shows the key points about behaviourism in the specification. Make sure that you are familiar with these.

Table 2.6 Key points of behaviourism

Antecedents	Stimuli that signal expected behaviour/responses
Consequences	Stimuli that encourage or reduce the occurrence of the behaviour
Positive and negative reinforcement	Can modify behaviour and learning (operant conditioning)
Continuity of reinforcements	Central to long-term associations Habit/response-forming
Association of experience (positive/negative reinforcement) with behavioural response	The student's motivation for learning is dependent on the teacher's response

Pedagogical approach and how it is applied

The specification gives three ways that behaviourism might be used when teaching.

1. Questioning

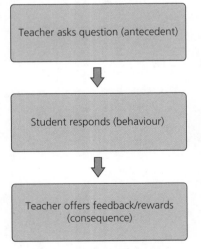

Figure 2.3 Questioning

2. Direct instruction

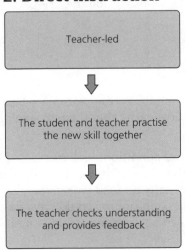

Figure 2.4 Direct instruction

Check your understanding and progress at **www.hoddereducation.co.uk/myrevisionnotes**

3. Mastery learning

Mastery learning is a new approach to teaching mathematics. It involves:

+ the **key instant recall facts (KIRF)** approach, which supports a solid grasp of key facts
+ a blend of direct instruction and practice
+ feedback provided by both teacher and peers.

Underpinning evidence

You may be asked to give an example of an experiment or a methodology that supports behaviourism as an approach. Five examples are given in the specification.

1   Pavlov's Dogs study: Pavlov showed that dogs could be trained to salivate in response to a bell rather than food. Dogs learnt to associate the bell with food.
2   Watson's Little Albert Experiment: Watson showed that phobias can be created if **punishers** (things to be avoided) are associated with an object or animal. Little Albert became afraid of rats because he learnt to associate rats with sudden loud noises.
3   Skinner's study of operant conditioning (Skinner box): Skinner showed the use of reinforcers, especially rewards, could shape the behaviour of rats and pigeons.
4   Ark Mathematics Mastery Project: This mathematics scheme was reviewed by the Education Endowment Foundation. It is based on the mastery learning approach.

> **Typical mistake**
>
> Linking Pavlov's and Watson's work to positive and negative reinforcement.

> **Exam tip**
>
> Unless specifically asked, do not refer to a theorist or an approach in a case study unless you are confident in your knowledge.

Cognitive constructivism

`REVISED`

Cognitive constructivism focuses on the way a person makes sense of new information by linking it to what they already know and then drawing new conclusions. The term schema is often used in relation to constructivism. It was used by Jean Piaget in his theory of cognitive development but has been more widely adopted. A **schema** (plural: schemata) is a way of thinking about something or doing something. A child may develop a schema that their key person belongs in the nursery, because this is where the child always sees them. When the child meets the key person in a shop, this is new information that will challenge the child's current thoughts and so may eventually change the child's schema about the key person.

Key features of this approach

Three features are given in the specification in relation to cognitive constructivism. (Note that these would not be universally recognised.)

1   Assimilation: learning builds on what students already know and can do.
2   Accommodation: knowledge is actively constructed through a process of discovery.
3   Sequential/Schematic: learning follows a sequence of stages.

Pedagogical approach and how it is applied

The specification gives three examples of how this approach could be used. You will need to remember these examples.

1   High scope: an early childhood programme that began in the USA.
  + Teachers provide challenging experiences and resources matched to their students' stages of development.
2   Project-based learning
  + Students engage in real life problems, such as designing a product, and are responsible for their choices, decisions and solutions.
3   Virtual reality
  + Using digital technology, learning takes place within a simulated real-world environment.

+ The student directly interacts with objects, tests out their ideas and instantly experiences the result of their actions.

Underpinning evidence

You may be asked to give an example of a theorist or a methodology that supports cognitive constructivism as an approach. There are three to remember.

1 Piaget's Four Stages of Development: Jean Piaget suggested that there were four stages of cognitive development. In each stage, children's thinking showed specific characteristics.
2 Bruner's Three Models of Representation: Jerome Bruner suggested that there are three ways of storing information (representation) and so learning: Enactive, Iconic and Symbolic. They develop sequentially in children between 0-7 years+. Once gained, more than one way can be used to problem solve or develop a new skill.
3 Kolb's Experiential Learning Cycle: David Kolb's theory of learning suggests that learning is a four-part cycle. Kolb highlights the importance of experience, reflection and experimentation.
4 Bloom's Taxonomy: Bloom helped to classify educational objectives into different levels and the skills associated with them. Teachers can use this taxonomy when designing programmes to help learners make progress.

Social constructivism

REVISED ◯

Social constructivism is based on the idea that children and young people learn through talking or doing things with adults or older children.

Key features of social constructivism

Three key features of social constructivism are given in the specification.

1 Active: children and young people's learning is a social process between teachers and peers.
2 Interactions: students' understanding and knowledge of the world is based on the quality of interactions with others.
3 Environment: the learning environment, home environment, culture and society can influence the quality of interactions.

Pedagogical approach and how it is applied

Make sure that you understand each point given in Table 2.7.

Table 2.7 Pedagogical approach of social constructivism

Approach	Application
Enquiry-based learning	The teacher plans activities to provoke curiosity and interaction between peers.
Modelling	The teacher models how to complete a task and the student observes before practising the task for themselves.
Flipped learning	+ The teacher provides material that students can access independently (for example, through a virtual learning environment). + The teacher observes and scaffolds activities during group learning. + The teacher differentiates content to make it accessible for all. + Formative assessments inform future teaching and learning.
Commentary	+ To develop students' vocabulary, the teacher talks through what they are doing. + The teacher demonstrates thinking skills, such as problem-solving.
Sustained shared thinking	+ The teacher and student share a genuine interest in an activity, conversation or discovery. + This can occur between individuals or in a group setting.
Reflection	The teacher talks about what went well and encourages the student to develop their own thinking.

Underpinning evidence

You may be asked to give an example of a theorist or a methodology that supports social constructivism as an approach. There are six examples to remember.

Table 2.8 Theories that support social constructivism

Theorist or approach	Explanation of theory
Bergmann and Sams' *Flip Your Classroom*	In this book, Bergmann and Sams explain how young people can look at videos or online lectures independently so that more time in the classroom is spent on discussion, group projects or getting support from teachers.
Bruner's Discovery Learning	As part of his work on cognitive development (see Cognitive constructivism), Jerome Bruner also focused on the importance of a problem-solving approach to learning in which adults support children's growing understanding.
Marion Dowling's *Young Children's Thinking*	Marion Dowling's book *Young Children's Thinking* describes how children's thinking develops from birth into Key Stage 1. She focuses on the role of adults, attachment and interactions with children.
Cathy Nutbrown's *Threads of Thinking*	Cathy Nutbrown's book *Threads of Thinking* shows the importance of schemas in children's play and the role of adults in observing and supporting children in their exploration of schemas.
The 30 Million Word Gap by Hart and Risley	Hart and Risley studied 42 families and concluded that some children heard 30 million more words by the age of 3 than their disadvantaged peers. Their work has prompted governments to focus on the importance of early language in the early years.
Vygotsky's Zone of Proximal Development	Lev Vygotsky was a pioneer of social constructivism. He suggested that children and young people could only go so far alone in their thinking and that learning should be a social process. He used the term 'Zone of Proximal Development' to describe the gap between what a child could achieve alone and what they could achieve with the support of adults and their peers.

Connectivism

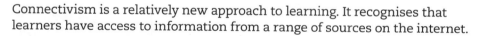
REVISED

Connectivism is a relatively new approach to learning. It recognises that learners have access to information from a range of sources on the internet.

Key features of the theory

The theory of connectivism is particularly associated with George Siemens. The five features given in the specification come from his paper 'Learning theory for the digital age'.

Table 2.9 Five features of connectivism from Siemens' 'Learning theory for the digital age'

Feature	Explanation of feature
Technology	+ Technology supports many of the learning sequences identified by earlier theory. + Students have greater access to online information, ideas and communities of learning.
Nodes	+ **Nodes** are objects (a person, a book, a webpage) that can be connected as part of a learning network. + Diversity of opinions and sources is key.
Links	+ Learning occurs when students make links between nodes, and they continue to make and maintain connections to form knowledge. + 'Know how' and 'know what' is replaced by 'know where to find knowledge'.
Currency	+ Knowledge is quickly obsolete and learning is a continual process. + Learning is more critical than knowing.
Informal	+ Formal learning no longer makes up the main way knowledge is acquired.

Pedagogical approach and how it is applied

The specification lists four ways of applying connectivism as an approach for learning. You will need to revise each of them.

1 Massive open online courses (MOOCs): these are online courses that can feature a mix of traditional course materials, user forums and communities of practice.
2 Social networking: allows information to be exchanged informally. Learners can talk to each other, but also to other people, and exchange information.
3 Gamification: based on the way that computer games are compelling, gamification allows tasks, fact learning and assignments to become competitive, interactive games.
4 Immersive learning: students are immersed in a task, working together to find, assess and make connections between information located in the digital world and the natural environment.

Underpinning evidence

You may be asked to give an example of an influential advocate of connectivism or a reference for this approach. There are three given in the specification. You will need to remember these.

1 Downes' 'Modernised learning delivery strategies': Downes carried out research with an organisation to improve their online delivery. The research looked at mobile devices, collaborative working and the use of virtual libraries to include links to videos and podcasts.
2 Siemens' 'Learning theory for the digital age' and 'Massive open online courses: Innovation in education?' Siemens' papers suggest that traditional ways of learning need to be overhauled. He outlined the principles of connectivism (see earlier). He also advocates peer learning networks and massive open online courses (MOOCs).
3 Lave and Wenger's Community of Practice: The Community of Practice is a theory that focuses on the social ways in which groups of people come together to learn, exchange ideas and explore information. A key difference to Siemens' and Downes' work is that groups may come together face-to-face, e.g. a book club.

Humanism

REVISED

Humanism, in the context of learning, is about recognising the needs, strengths, feelings and individuality of each child and young person. Humanism rejects the idea of a 'one-size fits all' approach to education.

Theory

The focus of humanism is **holistic learning** – seeing children and young people as individuals. The specification sets out six key features of holistic learning.

Holistic learning

1 Individuals construct knowledge in the context of their own unique feelings, values and experiences.
2 Feelings are as important as knowledge in the learning process.
3 The teacher's role is to facilitate rather than deliver learning.
4 Learning should be personalised to each individual student.
5 A student's person potential can only be fulfilled when their physical and affective needs have been met.
6 Humans are intentional and seek meaning, value and creativity.

> **Revision activity**
>
> Write down as many features of humanism as you can remember. After you have finished, check how well you did.

Pedagogical approach and how it is applied

Figure 2.5 shows the ways in which the humanist approach can be seen in education. There are three to remember.

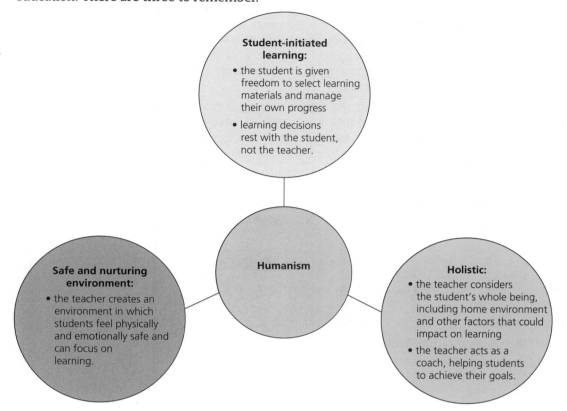

Student-initiated learning:
- the student is given freedom to select learning materials and manage their own progress
- learning decisions rest with the student, not the teacher.

Humanism

Safe and nurturing environment:
- the teacher creates an environment in which students feel physically and emotionally safe and can focus on learning.

Holistic:
- the teacher considers the student's whole being, including home environment and other factors that could impact on learning
- the teacher acts as a coach, helping students to achieve their goals.

Figure 2.5 The humanist approach in education

Underpinning evidence

You may be asked to give an example of an influential advocate of the humanist approach. Five are listed in the specification. You will need to remember them.

Table 2.10 Advocates of the humanist approach

Advocate	Features of this approach
Malaguzzi's '100 languages of a child'	Loris Malaguzzi was the inspiration behind the Reggio Emilia approach to early education. Features of the approach include: ✦ Teacher and children are partners in learning. ✦ Children can construct their own learning based on their interests. ✦ The environment is also a teacher. ✦ Children have many ways of thinking, playing, exploring and speaking (100 Languages). Loris Malaguzzi wrote the poem '100 languages of a child' as part of a touring exhibition to showcase the work of Reggio Emilia.
Paulo Freire's *Pedagogy of the oppressed*	Brazilian educator Paulo Freire's book *Pedagogy of the oppressed* criticises systems of education that are there to 'bank' knowledge in passive learners. Instead, he advocates a 'problem-posing' approach in which learners become critical thinkers and learn in partnership with their teachers.
Bronfenbrenner's ecological system	Urie Bronfenbrenner was interested in the processes and contexts that shape development. He proposed a model that demonstrates that there are wider influences on children and young people than just their immediate family or neighbourhood. ➡

Advocate	Features of this approach
United Nations Convention on the Rights of the Child 1989	The UNCRC is a list of 45 rights that all children and young people should have regardless of where they live or their personal circumstances. Some of the articles are relevant to the humanist pedagogy. Article 12 states 'Every child has the right to express their views, feelings and wishes in all matters affecting them, and to have their views considered and taken seriously'. Article 29 about education states 'Education must develop every child's personality, talents and abilities to the full. It must encourage the child's respect for human rights, as well as respect for their parents, their own and other cultures, and the environment.'
Maslow's hierarchy of needs	Abraham Maslow's hierarchy of needs proposes that there is an order of needs which must be met. His model is often shown in a triangle. At the base of the triangle are the basic needs, such as food and shelter. In terms of education, his theory would suggest that children and young people cannot achieve their potential until all their needs have been met.
Carl Rogers' *Freedom to Learn*	In his book *Freedom to learn*, Carl Rogers outlines the importance of meaningful learning for children and young people. This is often referred to as **experiential learning**, where the needs and wants of the learner are the focus. As part of this theory, Carl Rogers stresses the importance of a positive climate in which learning takes place.

Now test yourself

TESTED ◯

15 Which of the six perspectives on humanism focuses on the importance of meeting learners' basic needs as a priority?

16 Give one feature of behaviourism.

17 Explain what is meant by cognitive constructivism.

18 Which theory focuses on the role of social interactions in guiding learning?

Revision activity

Look at the following theoretical approaches to learning. For each approach consider to what extent learning is likely to be highly structured by adults or chosen by children and young people.

+ Behaviourism
+ Humanism
+ Cognitive constructivism
+ Social constructivism
+ Connectivism

Exam-style question

6 You are invited to visit a classroom. The pupils are facing the front and looking at a screen. The teacher tells the pupils that they will be learning about turnover, profit and loss. The teacher gives a short explanation and then puts an exercise on the screen and tells the pupils to write it down and complete it. The pupils work individually. The teacher walks around to assist anyone who is finding the task difficult. The pupils are given a test at the end of the lesson to see whether they have understood the concept.

After break, the pupils are reminded of the concept that they were taught. They are asked to get into pairs or groups. They are asked to give examples of businesses that require a high turnover in order to generate a profit, with a view to creating a presentation for the rest of the group. They are asked to think about where they might get the information and encouraged to use the internet or to talk to local businesses. The pupils can decide for themselves how best to present the information and use their time. The teacher is on hand to provide advice and guidance, but the focus is on encouraging pupils to think for themselves.

A Identify which theoretical approaches are being used. [2]

B Explain how each approach to learning is being used to support students' learning. [4]

C Evaluate how effective this way of working might be in supporting learning. [6]

Check your understanding and progress at **www.hoddereducation.co.uk/myrevisionnotes**

2.4 How metacognition supports children and young people to manage their own learning

Metacognition is being aware of thought processes and how to regulate them. A good example of this: you might tell yourself to reread some information, as you are aware that you have not understood it.

Impact of metacognition

REVISED ●

You will need to understand how metacognition helps children to manage their own learning and how it impacts on children's and young people's education and achievement.

The NCFE specification lists three ways in which metacognition supports children and young people to manage their own learning:

1 Identifying the strengths and areas for development in their own learning
2 Using cognitive strategies to 'construct' knowledge
3 Using metacognitive strategies to regulate and evaluate their own learning.

Identifying the strengths and areas for development in their own learning

When children and young people can identify where they need to practise, concentrate more or ask for help, they can make better progress with their learning. This requires that they can identify their strengths and also the areas where they need to work further.

Using cognitive strategies to 'construct' knowledge

This is about connecting pieces of existing knowledge to a new situation to create new knowledge. A child can count to ten and recognise the number four. When it is his birthday, he notices a card with the number four on it. He says, 'I am four and that is why this card has the number four on it. Next year, I will have a card with the number five on it.'

Using metacognitive strategies to regulate and evaluate their own learning

There are many metacognitive strategies that can be used to help with learning. A child or young person might think about ways to remember an important fact, such as linking the fact that 13 is a prime number to unlucky Friday the 13th, or visualising a hidden 'r' popping out of in front of the 'p' in 'surprise' when remembering how to spell it.

Children and young people can also ask themselves whether they understand or can remember what they need to learn. In this way they can evaluate their learning and think about what they need to do further.

Understand how metacognition positively impacts on children's and young people's education and achievement

REVISED ●

There are six ways in which metacognition can help children and young people to achieve:

1 building up a set of transferable strategies and skills that they can apply to new subjects and situations

37

2 better preparing for assessments
3 monitoring their own understanding
4 identifying barriers to their own learning and actively minimising them
5 learning from mistakes in order to avoid them in the future
6 adapting their learning strategies as appropriate to the task.

Now test yourself

19 How does metacognition help children and young people identify their strengths and weaknesses?

20 Give an example of how a metacognition strategy might be used to learn from a mistake.

21 Explain how metacognition strategies can impact children's and young people's progress.

TESTED

Exam-style question

7 Maisie is revising for a maths test. She reviews the topics that need to be revised. Next to each topic, she puts a tick if she is confident, a cross if she knows she will need to work hard on it or a question mark if there are some elements that need working on.

While revising, she looks at the feedback that she has been given in order to prevent herself from making the same errors. Maisie tests herself repeatedly on the areas in which she has performed badly in the past. To help her remember one concept, she even draws a picture that she hopes will help to trigger her memory. When Maisie gets her results, she is pleased that her hard work has paid off.

Analyse the ways in which metacognition strategies have played a part in Maisie's revision. [6]

2.5 How practitioners provide effective feedback and why it is important in supporting educational development

Feedback is information that practitioners give to children and young people. This can be through written comments as well as verbally. Effective feedback helps children and young people to:

+ make progress with their learning and development, but also their behaviour
+ know what they are doing well as well as areas and strategies to make improvements.

There is a link between effective feedback and metacognition. If the process of effective feedback is carried out with children and young people, they can learn how to evaluate their own learning. This can become a metacognition strategy that they use independently.

You need to learn the six features that make feedback effective and why they matter.

Table 2.11 Six features that make feedback effective

Feature of effective feedback	Why it matters
Timely	To support clarity, motivation and retention of information.
Clear and detailed	Children/young people can identify precisely what they need to improve. This in turn can help them achieve success and so help them to remain motivated.
Relevant to criteria	Children/young people can understand how they have achieved the outcomes, and where they still need to develop.
Action-orientated	Children/young people have specific goals for the future and know what they should continue to do.
Ongoing	Children/young people can revisit and re-evaluate learning as part of a continuous process.
Interactive	Ensures clarity through a dialogue between the teacher/student/peers.

Revision activity

Draw a spider diagram with 'Features of effective feedback' in the centre. Draw six legs, giving a feature for each leg. Afterwards, check your diagram against Table 2.8.

Check your understanding and progress at **www.hoddereducation.co.uk/myrevisionnotes**

Now test yourself   TESTED ○

22 Why is 'timely' an important feature of effective feedback?

23 Explain the importance to children and young people of involving them in feedback.

24 Identify why clear and detailed feedback might impact on a young person's progress.

Exam-style question

8 Tia's teacher has handed her homework back. Her mark is 8/10. The only comment on the work is 'good'.

Explain why the lack of effective feedback might affect Tia's progress in this subject.

[4]

2.6 Why up-to-date and appropriate technology is important to effectively support educational development

For this outcome, you need to be able to explain the ways in which technology might be used to support development.

Nine ways of using technology are given. You can divide these into three broad areas:
+ Using technology for professional and administrative purposes.
+ Supporting learning and teaching.
+ Teaching children/young people how to use the internet effectively and safely.

Using technology for professional and administrative purposes

REVISED ○

These two ways of using technology support the work of the teacher/practitioner:
1 Monitoring children's/young people's progress, for example, predicting grades; analysing the results of recent assessments.
2 Easily sharing information, for example, sharing information within a setting; sharing photos with parents in early years settings.

Supporting learning and teaching

REVISED ○

These three ways show how technology might be used directly with children or young people to support learning and teaching:
3 Using a variety of media to introduce and explore a topic, for example, a digital camera.
4 Planning and designing suitable online and offline learning materials and assessments, for example, identifying maths games to practise skills.
5 Making learning accessible for children/young people with SEND, for example, providing large-print keyboards or voice-activated writing software.

Making links

Read the section in Element 11 about augmentative and alternative communication (AAC). Can you give a practical example of how technology might be used to help a young person who has difficulty talking?

39

Teaching children/young people how to use the internet effectively and safely

REVISED ●

These four ways are mainly about teaching children and young people about how to use the internet effectively and safely:

6 Communicating and collaborating safely with children/young people online, for example, understanding the effects of writing inappropriate messages.

7 Equipping children/young people to navigate a vast amount of information and evaluate the validity of sources, for example, identifying false information.

8 Modelling legal, ethical and secure methods of accessing/using online data and media, for example, teaching the importance of passwords and how to create secure ones.

9 Helping to prepare children/young people for future careers and digital citizenship, for example, showing how the internet can be used to gain information and develop new knowledge.

Revision activity

Read this section again. Copy and complete the table below. For each area, write the different ways in which technology might be used. Part of the table has been started for you.

Typical mistake

Don't give an example of using technology that is inappropriate for the situation, for example, suggesting that babies use the internet.

Purpose	How it can be used	Example
Using technology for professional and administrative purposes	1 *Monitoring children's/ young people's progress*	*Predicting grades, analysing the results of recent assessments*
	2 *Easily sharing information*	
Supporting learning and teaching	3	
	4	
	5	
Teaching children/young people how to use the internet effectively and safely	6	
	7	
	8	
	9	

2.7 How personal, educational and environmental factors may affect engagement and development in reading, literacy and mathematics

A range of factors can affect children's/young people's interest and progress in reading, literacy and mathematics, both positively but also negatively. These factors fall into three categories:

1 personal
2 educational
3 environmental.

Exam tip

Read questions carefully as this outcome is focused only on reading, literacy and mathematics. Make sure that your answer reflects this.

Personal factors

REVISED ●

There are eight personal factors listed in the specification that can affect reading, literacy and mathematics. To make it easier to revise, you can subdivide them into three broad areas.

Cognition, language, disability and health

This area covers the following factors:

+ level of cognitive and language development – being able to remember information, having strong vocabulary
+ SEND – such as attention deficit hyperactivity disorder (ADHD), sight problems
+ bilingualism and/or EAL – this particularly affects refugees
+ physical health and wellbeing – such as asthma, childhood cancer, family bereavement.

To learn to read, write and develop mathematic skills requires a certain level of thinking, memory (**cognition**), and language and vocabulary. Children and young people with learning difficulties or a disability may need additional support.

Where a child or young person is new to English, they will also need support until they are speaking fluently and have the vocabulary to follow what is being taught.

Where a child or young person has repeated absences because of a medical condition or emotional difficulties, they may miss out on teaching.

Some physical health difficulties such as eczema and emotional difficulties such as bereavement may also make it hard for a child or young person to focus on a lesson.

Interest and feelings

This area covers the following personal factors:

+ motivation and interest
+ confidence to try without fear of failure.

Emotions can have an impact on the development of reading, writing and mathematics.

Children and young people have to be interested in learning, but also confident enough to cope when they make mistakes.

Life circumstances

This area covers the following factors:

1 Socio-economic circumstances:
    + Research shows that children and young people from high-income and educated households are more likely to make progress in reading, literacy and mathematics.
    + Parents are more likely to buy resources to help their children, such as software programs and textbooks, or may even hire a tutor.
    + Parents with higher levels of education are more confident in supporting their children with homework and also raising concerns if their child is not making progress.
2 Previous experiences or support:
    + Children and young people who have had access to books, writing materials and mathematical games and activities from a young age are more likely to be interested in reading and maths.
    + Children and young people who have had positive experiences of reading, literacy and mathematics are more likely to enjoy activities. They are likely to persevere and practise more.

> **Socio-economic circumstances** The income and education level of a household.

Educational factors

Table 2.12 How educational factors affect engagement and development

Factor	Explanation	Examples
Quality of teaching and support	Adult time and support is a key factor when learning to read, write and develop mathematical concepts. Some children and young people get extra help at home – such as parents who hear their children read – and this gives them a significant advantage.	+ Careful assessment to know when a concept has been mastered or when more support is needed. + Finding appealing ways to present the skills that are needed. + A good relationship with the child or young person.
Age- and stage-appropriate materials	Resources such as reading scheme books and board games can support teaching. If the resources are not age-appropriate, they will not be effective. Some parents are able to afford a wide variety of age-appropriate books, toys and other educational resources which can give their children an advantage. Others will not be able to afford to provide this variety.	+ Threading beads to help four-year-olds with counting and making patterns. + Weighing scales for KS2 children to learn to estimate and then measure different weights. + Good selection of books to encourage young people to read widely.
Use of aids and adaptations	Some children and young people may need resources adapted in order to help them learn. This might be because of a learning disability or medical condition, e.g. sight problems.	+ Audio books to help young people who find reading difficult. + Triangular pens to help with writing grip. + Large-print keyboard to help a young person with sight problems.
Use of **synthetic phonics**	This systematic approach to teaching reading and writing is used in Reception and KS1. It is thought to be effective for many children.	+ Structured teaching sessions to introduce Reception children to letter shapes and corresponding sounds. + Careful assessment to check progress and to plan further activities.

Revision activity

Copy and complete this table. For each of these educational factors, give an example of what might happen if they were not available for a child or young person. The first example is given for you.

Educational factor	Effect of unavailability of the factor
Quality of teaching and support	*If adults do not teach and support well, a young person may not be able to get a qualification.*
Age- and stage-appropriate materials	
Use of aids and adaptations	
Use of synthetic phonics	

> **Synthetic phonics** A system of teaching reading and writing which involves breaking down the sounds in words to their smallest components, e.g. s-t-i-ck-er.

Environmental factors

Three main environmental factors are listed which may affect engagement and development. These are about where children and young people grow up and the experiences that they have. See Figure 2.5.

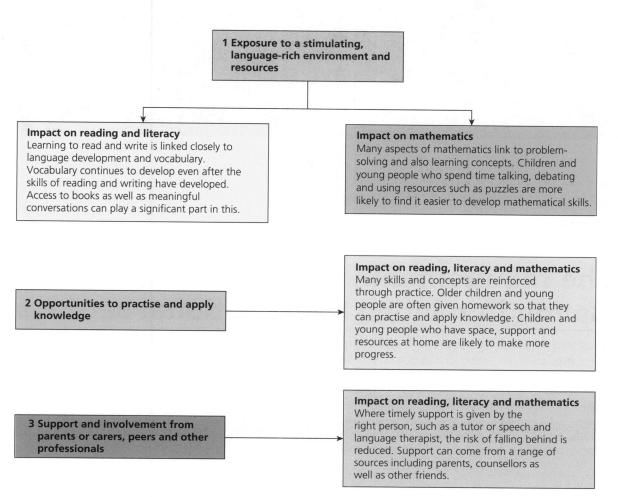

Figure 2.6 Environmental factors

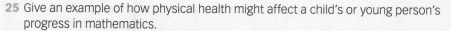

Now test yourself   TESTED ◯

25 Give an example of how physical health might affect a child's or young person's progress in mathematics.

26 Explain why quality teaching and support can impact progress with reading, literacy and mathematics.

27 How can a language-rich environment positively impact a child's or young person's literacy skills?

Exam-style question

9   Harrison lives in a low-income household. Money is tight and this means that toys, books and opportunities for outings and activities are scarce.

Harrison has a language disorder and is seen regularly by a speech and language therapist. Harrison attends a primary school which has recently had an 'inadequate' judgement for quality of education. His teacher is not knowledgeable about how to teach reading and is disorganised. The teacher also struggles to manage the behaviour of some of the other children which leads to disruption during lessons. Harrison finds that the teacher often appears bad-tempered and lacks patience. Some lessons are also very boring because the children can only sit and listen, and there is a lot of rote learning.

A   Identify a range of factors that might affect Harrison's progress in school. [4]

B   With reference to the case study, discuss the role of teachers and practitioners in supporting children's and young people's education. [6]

43

3 Safeguarding, health and safety and wellbeing

Safeguarding is a key aspect of your role. All those who work with children and young people have a responsibility to keep them safe and free from harm.

> **Safeguarding** Action taken to promote the welfare of children and protect them from harm.

3.1 The requirements and purpose of legislation in relation to educational settings

The first thing you will need to know about and understand is the relevant legislation and guidance, so that you can see how it affects what happens in different settings.

Table 3.1 Legal requirements and guidance

Legislation	Why it is relevant
Health and Safety at Work Act 1974	This Act relates to how health and safety is managed in the setting, e.g. reporting hazards, using safety equipment, keeping yourself and others safe.
Children Act 2004	This Act was set up to support multi-agency working to keep children safe. It also ensures that parents and all those who work with children and young people are able to safeguard and promote the welfare of children. It includes two specific sections that focus on safeguarding: ✦ Section 17 – services must be put in place by local authorities to 'safeguard and promote the welfare of children within their area who are in need'. ✦ Section 47 – the local authority has a duty to investigate instances where it has 'reasonable cause to suspect that a child is suffering, or likely to suffer, significant harm'.
Female Genital Mutilation (FGM) Act 2003	Includes provisions intended to protect young girls and be vigilant/know the signs to look out for that may indicate risk of FGM. Under this Act it is an offence to fail to protect a girl from such a risk.
Safeguarding Vulnerable Groups Act 2006	Aims to prevent unsuitable people from working with children and young people and vulnerable adults. Through this the CRB (now **DBS check**) was set up for checking the background of everyone working with vulnerable groups.
Children and Families Act (Part 3: Children and young people with special educational needs (SEN) and disabilities) 2014	This Act was set up to improve services for children. Parents and families have more control over their child's welfare. The Act sets out the requirement for an **Education, Health and Care Plan (EHCP)** for children and young people with **SEND**.
Counter Terrorism and Security Act 2015	This Act was brought in to respond to the risk of terrorism. It was introduced to ensure that relevant authorities consider the need to prevent people from being drawn into terrorism and act to prevent radicalisation. This is also called the Prevent duty.
Data Protection Act 2018	This legislation is relevant to all organisations that record, store and share information. Educational settings will need to store information and manage how they do this to maintain confidentiality. (See also Section 3.2.)

> **DBS check** The DBS (Disclosure and Barring Service – formerly CRB) check is a legal requirement for those working with children and young people. It applies to the health and social care sectors and those working in education and early years.

Check your understanding and progress at **www.hoddereducation.co.uk/myrevisionnotes**

Education, Health and Care plan (EHCP) A document which sets out the provision needed for a child or young person who has SEND.

SEND (or SEN) 'A child or young person has SEN if they have a learning difficulty or disability which calls for special educational provision to be made for him or her' (SEND Code of Practice 2015).

Revision activity

Draw a spider diagram with 'Legislation' in the centre and a piece of legislation on each leg.
+ See how many pieces of legislation you can remember.
+ Include dates if you can.
+ Check your answers and add those you missed.

Now test yourself

TESTED ◯

1 Which legislation aims to improve services for vulnerable children and sets out the requirement for an Education, Health and Care Plan?
2 How does the Data Protection Act 2018 impact on how organisations store information?
3 Which Act was introduced to ensure that relevant authorities act to prevent children and young people from being drawn into terrorism?

3.2 How statutory guidance informs policies and procedures in educational settings

By law, your setting will need to have policies and procedures in place for the protection of children and young people and everybody who works in or visits the setting, as well as the personal data it handles. In addition to knowing about the legislation, you need to make links to your setting's policies and procedures, and to school/early years policies.

Table 3.2 Links between legislation and the setting's policies and procedures

Name and context of guidance	Relevant policy/procedure in educational settings
Health and Safety	
Health and safety: responsibilities and duties for schools 2021	This document outlines the considerations that schools must have regarding health and safety, in order to keep pupils safe in school and when taking part in out-of-school activities. It will directly relate to the school's Health and Safety Policy and to the procedures for risk assessment.
EYFS Welfare Requirements	These requirements form part of the EYFS Statutory framework. They outline what early years settings must do to keep children safe and well. This will relate to the Early Years Policy as well as the Safeguarding/Child protection and Health and Safety policies.
Security	
Prevent Duty Guidance 2021	Prevent refers to the Counter Terrorism and Security Act 2015 and aims to prevent young people from being drawn into terrorism. The Safeguarding or Prevent policy should outline the level of risk of this occurring in an organisation or area. Schools and early years settings may also refer to it in their IT policy.
Confidentiality of information	
Data Protection Act 2018/UK General Data Protection Regulation (UK GDPR)	The Data Protection Act 2018 and the UK GDPR together form the UK's version of the GDPR legislation from the European Union. They inform the policies and procedures that organisations must put in place around recording, storing and sharing information. This means that all those who follow the UK GDPR must adhere to seven principles regarding information, including handling data in a secure way to prevent unauthorised use, access, loss or damage. It relates to the organisation's Data Protection and Confidentiality policies. It may also relate to the IT policy.
Safeguarding and promoting the welfare of children and young people	
Supporting pupils at school with medical conditions 2015	This guidance relates to the Safeguarding policy and is specifically for schools, as early years settings should refer to the EYFs framework. As well as ensuring that pupils with medical conditions are supported effectively, it points out that these pupils may be more vulnerable to abuse due to their needs. It also relates to the Administration of Medicines policy.

45

Name and context of guidance	Relevant policy/procedure in educational settings
Guidance for safer working practice for those working with children and young people in education settings 2022	This is a non-statutory document from the Safer Recruitment Consortium that should be read alongside the DfE document 'Keeping children safe in education 2019'. It sets out the need for a staff code of conduct and gives practical advice for standards of behaviour that are expected from those who work with children and young people.
Working together to Safeguard children 2018	This guidance relates to the Safeguarding policy and sets out how different agencies can work together to: + protect children and young people + support their welfare.
Multi-agency statutory guidance on female genital mutilation 2020	This guidance relates to the Safeguarding policy. It provides information and support for safeguarding girls from FGM. It also sets out the requirements of the legislation and how to report concerns.
Keeping children safe in education 2022	This statutory guidance relates to the Safeguarding and/or Child protection and Behaviour policy. It is for maintained nursery schools, schools and colleges including independent and special schools and Pupil Referral Units (PRUs). It sets out: + how organisations should support the safeguarding of children and young people + the role of all staff in protecting children and young people + what to do if they have concerns and need to refer these to the police and/or social care. Local Safeguarding partners were put in place as defined by the Children and Social Work Act 2017 to replace LSCBs (Local Safeguarding Children Boards.)

Now test yourself   TESTED ○

4   How does the EYFS statutory framework link to health and safety?

5   Which policies or procedures does Keeping children safe in education 2021 relate to?

Data Protection Act (DPA) 2018, UK General Data Protection Regulation (UK GDPR)

REVISED ○

Together with the DPA, the UK GDPR is the UK's version of the GDPR legislation from the European Union. These pieces of legislation inform the policies and procedures which organisations must have in place around recording, storing and sharing information. This means that all those who follow the UK GDPR must adhere to seven principles with regard to information:

1   Obtain and keep it fairly, lawfully and transparently.
2   Use it only for the specified purpose and inform people what this purpose is.
3   Only collect the minimum amount of data needed.
4   Ensure it is accurate and up to date, and do not keep it for longer than necessary.
5   Ensure the safe disposal of personal data after use.
6   Handle it in a secure way to prevent unauthorised use, access, loss or damage.
7   Keep documentation and policies regarding data collection within the principles of UK GDPR.

Typical mistake

Don't think that you can never share information. Safeguarding policies may mean that staff have to share information about children or young people with colleagues and social services in order to protect them.

Now test yourself   TESTED ○

6   Name four of the UK GDPR principles.

Exam-style question

1 What is the purpose of the Prevent Duty Guidance? Choose one option. [1]
   A To prevent schools and early years settings from employing those who might cause sexual abuse
   B To prevent children and young people from being drawn into terrorism
   C To prevent schools and early years settings from sharing data
   D To prevent children and young people from bullying each other

3.3 The importance of children's and young people's emotional health and its impact on overall wellbeing

Children's and young people's emotional health has been recognised as having a direct impact on their learning and development as well as their wellbeing. Mental health problems such as self-harm and depression have increased in recent years.

The importance of children's and young people's personal circumstances in relation to their holistic wellbeing

Children's and young people's personal circumstances and their holistic wellbeing are closely related. Personal circumstances include the quality of relationships with parents or carers as well as key adults and peers in their lives, such as early years practitioners, teachers and friends. Personal circumstances also include whether children and young people have their physical needs met so that they are safe and healthy. Children and young people also need opportunities to play, be creative and also stimulated. Where children's and young people's overall needs are being met, they are more likely to make strong relationships with others, enjoy learning and stay healthy.

The significance of emotional health for positive relationships

Our emotional health is about how we think and feel; it determines how we deal with emotions and experiences, or how we self-regulate. It also affects how we deal with the emotions of others. Children and young people who have good emotional health are more likely to develop strong relationships with others, which in turn helps them to be resilient and develop a positive self-identity (see further Unit 7).

> **Self-regulation** Our ability to control our own emotions, thoughts and behaviour, adjust to changing situations and cope with unexpected stress.

> **Making links**
> This links to Element 5: Parents, families and carers. List three ways that schools and early years settings can work with parents to support children's and young people's holistic wellbeing.

3.4 The difference between a child or young person 'at risk' and 'in need'

A child or young person at risk is one who is vulnerable to abuse or harm. The abuse may be happening (or may not be), or it may be at risk of happening for different reasons (see Section 3.5 for more detail).

A child or person in need is defined by law as a person under 18 who needs extra support to improve their opportunities. This may be given through the local authority due to a child's medical or physical need, such as being a looked after child (LAC).

> **Looked after child (LAC)** A child who has been in the care of their local authority for more than 24 hours.

47

Mandatory reporting requirements to escalate concerns that a child or young person is in need or at risk

For professionals working with children and young people, one of the key responsibilities is to keep them safe and free from harm. Any concerns that a child or young person is in need or at risk must be reported by law.

The documents 'Keeping children safe in education' and 'What to do if you are worried a child is being abused – advice for practitioners' give detailed information about how staff should meet their responsibilities under legislation. They state that if a member of staff has any concerns about a child, they should act on them immediately following the setting's safeguarding policy. This will involve reporting to the DSL and giving as much information as possible.

> **DSL (Designated Safeguarding Lead)**
> Person in a school or setting who is responsible for all safeguarding issues.

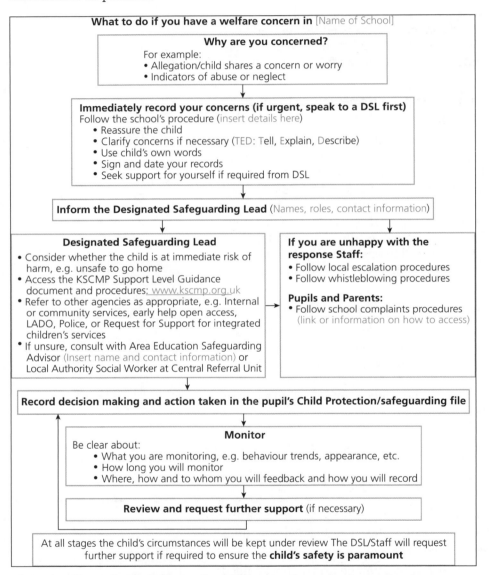

Figure 3.1 Example of a safeguarding/child protection policy for a school

Source: KELSI www.kelsi.org.uk/__data/assets/pdf_file/0020/66008/Child-Protection-Exemplar-Policy-for-schools.pdf

Check your understanding and progress at **www.hoddereducation.co.uk/myrevisionnotes**

Revision activity

Using the most up-to-date version of 'Keeping children safe in education', identify what practitioners should do in the following situations:
✚ if they have concerns about a child or young person
✚ how they should report and record their concerns
✚ where they should go for additional advice and support.

Now test yourself   TESTED

7   What does it mean if a child is described as 'in need'?
8   What policy should you follow if you have concerns about a child or young person?

3.5 Factors that may indicate that a child or young person is in danger or at risk of abuse

Children and young people may be in danger or at risk of different types of abuse. This is normally categorised in one of the following ways. You should remember that it is possible to be the victim of more than one of these types of abuse:

✚ **Physical abuse** – when someone is physically harmed.
✚ **Emotional abuse** – when someone is continually emotionally mistreated.
✚ **Sexual abuse** – when someone is forced to take part in sexual activity. This includes child sexual exploitation (CSE).
✚ **Neglect** – when a baby's, child's or young person's needs are persistently not being met.
✚ **Domestic abuse** – when there is violent behaviour perpetrated by members of the same household.
✚ **Bullying and cyber-bullying** – when a child or young person is the victim of bullying or cyber-bullying by their peers.
✚ **Child criminal exploitation (CCE)** – when a child or young person is trafficked or exploited and made to commit crimes, for example, as part of a gang.

According to the World Health Organization (WHO), research shows that there is often a link between a child's or young person's environment and risk factors which may indicate that they are more in danger or at risk. These are divided into individual, parental and environmental factors.

Making links

For EY this links to PO4; for AT it links to PO3. List the indicators for physical and emotional abuse.

Table 3.3 Factors indicating that children and young people might be in danger or at risk

Type of factor	The impact of this factor on the child or young person
Individual factors (relating to the child or young person)	✚ The child or young person has a physical or developmental disability – they may be unable to stop the abuser/more vulnerable or have less understanding/less likely to tell others. ✚ The child or young person has been impacted by an abusive relationship – abuse is already in the home. ✚ There is a lack of secure attachment with their parent or carer – lack of attachment will increase the likelihood of abuse.
Parental factors (relating to the child's or young person's parents)	✚ Parent has already abused or been abused as a child or young person – more likely to abuse. ✚ Parents have unrealistic expectations of child – uninformed or do not know about child development. ✚ Parents need support with parenting skills, such as managing dietary or health needs. ✚ Parental isolation – those who have less support with their parenting are more likely to abuse. ✚ Parental mental illness. ✚ Parental drug or alcohol abuse – abuse may stem from low self-esteem and lack of control.
Environmental factors (relating to the child's or young person's environment)	✚ Overcrowding in the home – increased stress levels. ✚ Poverty or lack of opportunity to improve resource. ✚ Domestic violence – violence is already in the home.

49

Exam tip

If you are answering a question about different risk factors and how they affect the likelihood that a child or young person may suffer abuse, you must be specific about why this may be the case. For example, a child or young person from an overcrowded home may be more likely to be abused because stress levels are higher.

Now test yourself | TESTED ◯

9 Name three forms of abuse.

10 How might individual factors affect the danger or risk of abuse?

11 What is meant by environmental factors affecting the risk of abuse? Give one example of an environmental factor.

3.6 The legal definition of a position of trust, as defined by the Sexual Offences (Amendment) Act 2000, and how power and influence can be used and abused

The Sexual Offences (Amendment) Act 2000 states that it is an offence for someone over 18 to engage in sexual activity with someone under that age when they are in a position of trust.

All adults who work with children and young people should be aware that they are in this position – they may be responsible for children or young people who are in:

+ a care home, are in residential care or are fostered
+ full-time education in which the older person is involved in caring for them
+ a hospital, children's home or residential establishment that cares for children with physical or learning disabilities, mental illness or behavioural problems.

Table 3.4 gives examples of how adults may use their position in a negative way.

Table 3.4 How adults may use their position in a negative way

How a position of trust might be abused by an adult	What this might involve
Taking advantage of an individual	Those in a position of trust may use their influence to exploit a child or young person for their own benefit.
Gaining unauthorised access to private or sensitive information for their own or others' advantage	Adults may look at sensitive information which they are not entitled to do, in order to find out more about the child or young person for their own advantage.
Manipulating an individual	Those in a position of power may try to manipulate a child or young person by controlling them and using their position to get what they want.
Using a position of trust to bully, humiliate or undermine	Adults may use their position to use verbal abuse in ways which make the child or young person feel humiliated or bullied.
Threatening punishment for non-compliance with unreasonable demands	Adults may threaten a child or young person by telling them that they will punish them if they do not do what they have asked them to.

Now test yourself | TESTED ◯

12 What is the legal definition of a position of trust?

13 Identify three ways in which an adult might abuse their position.

Check your understanding and progress at **www.hoddereducation.co.uk/myrevisionnotes**

3.7 Grooming: an individual developing a relationship, trust and emotional connection with a child or young person so that they can manipulate, exploit and abuse them

Sadly, in some rare cases, adults may groom children or young people so that they can manipulate, abuse or exploit them. This may take place in-person or online and can often be carried out by members of the child's close family or social circle.

Table 3.5 How children could be groomed or exploited

Method of grooming	How this may occur
By adults in a position of trust	Adults in a position of trust who work with children or young people may take advantage of the trust which has been placed in them (see Section 3.6).
By interfamilial abuse	This is grooming by a family member. A young child will trust those closest to them and may not know that what is happening is wrong.
Through the use of inappropriate games	Groomers might tell a young child that they are going to play a game in order to gain their trust; this may then be inappropriate.
Through online materials/communication	Older children may receive text messages or online material from groomers. They may be complimented or flattered to make them feel good before the abuse takes place.
Through observing sexual behaviour of others/being exposed to pornographic content	The child or young person may be forced to watch others engaging in sexual behaviour, either in person or through pornography.
Through threats of harm to the individual or family	This happens when groomers use blackmail so that the child or young person will not tell anyone about what is happening.
County lines	County lines refers to the mobile phone lines which are used to order the drugs from cities to towns and rural areas. Vulnerable children and young people are targeted by drug dealers to deliver the drugs. They may befriend or threaten the child or young person.

If you have any concerns about an individual in your setting, you should follow the setting's whistleblowing policy.

Whistleblowing Reporting a co-worker for something that is wrong and that affects others.

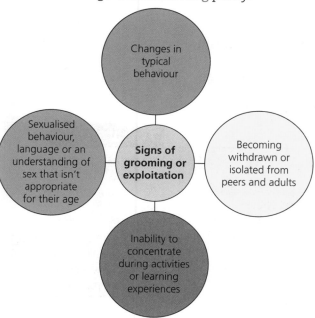

Figure 3.2 Signs of grooming or exploitation

Now test yourself

14 Give two signs of grooming or exploitation.

15 What are your responsibilities when it comes to raising concerns about grooming or exploitation?

TESTED ○

51

Appropriate action to take when grooming or abuse is suspected

In situations where you suspect abuse or grooming, it is important to follow the correct procedures so that the child is protected as soon as possible. This means:

+ Following the safeguarding policies and procedures of your setting.
+ Reporting immediately to the setting's Designated Safeguarding Lead. All staff should be aware who this person is in their setting.
+ Liaising with Local Authority Designated Officer (LADO), as appropriate.
+ Remaining calm and professional (if disclosures are made). This means making sure that you keep calm when speaking to the child or young person about what they have told you.
+ Maintaining accurate and coherent records and reports. Follow your setting's confidentiality and safeguarding policies and record only what has been said or seen as soon as possible.
+ Sharing information only when required/maintaining confidentiality. Only share information or concerns with your setting's DSL.

> **Disclosure** Being told about something; in this situation a disclosure of grooming or abuse.

Exam-style question

2 You are working in a Year 2 class with a child who has told you that his stepbrother has made him do something which causes you concern.

   A Which policy would you need to refer to so that you would know what to do? [1]

   B What might you say to the child? [2]

3.8 The range of indicators that an adult in a setting may have inappropriate relationships with children and young people

Although very rare, it is possible that an adult in a setting may develop an inappropriate relationship with a child or young person. You should be aware of any signs that this may be taking place and be prepared to act on this if so. You may notice that they are:

+ being over-affectionate or flirtatious, giving gifts or showing favouritism
+ spending time alone with a child or young person
+ making friends with a child's or young person's parents and/or visiting them at home
+ using private messages or social media to communicate with a child or young person.

> **Typical mistake**
>
> Do not accept invitations to connect with children or young people privately on social media. It is *never* a good idea to communicate with a child or young person privately. This is likely to be covered in your setting's safeguarding policy.

Exam-style question

3 Tasha is a teaching assistant in a girls' secondary school and has noticed that one of the male teachers is flirting and being over-familiar with several of the girls. She has asked other staff if they have noticed his behaviour, but she has only been at the school for a few months and is too nervous to say anything to managers.

   A Is this the correct course of action? [1]

   B Explain how you would respond if Tasha spoke to you about what she has noticed? [4]

How practitioners deal with suspected abuse in line with the educational setting's codes of conduct

Safeguarding concerns should always be acted on immediately. The kind of actions which should be taken are listed below:

+ Observing and recording as appropriate – always note down any concerns including the date/time, what was observed or what the child or young person has said. The information should then be reported and stored securely.
+ Following organisational policies and procedures for child protection – making sure each step in the policy is followed carefully.
+ Following procedures set out by the local safeguarding partnership – this will mean following your setting's policy and will also include what to do outside office hours.
+ Following accurate lines of reporting in a timely manner – act quickly and report to the DSL.
+ Maintaining confidential boundaries – remain professional and only talk to those who need to know about the situation.
+ Contacting the police if a child or young person is in immediate danger – always call 999 in this situation.

> **Local safeguarding partnerships** Statutory local organisations set up to promote the safeguarding and welfare of children and young people and to coordinate local healthcare, education and local authority providers.

> **Exam tip**
>
> If a question asks you to explain or describe what you would do, you will need to give an answer which is longer than one word.
> + 'Explain' means that you should say what you would do and why.
> + 'Describe' means that you should give the characteristics of something.

> **Now test yourself**
>
> TESTED
>
> **16** What is the function of the local safeguarding partnership?
>
> **17** Explain what you would do if you had concerns about another member of staff.

3.9 How abuse, neglect, bullying, persecution and violence may impact on development and behaviour

Types of abuse such as neglect, bullying, persecution and violence will have an impact on the development, behaviour and future prospects of a child or young person if not addressed. If the abuse continues in the long term, it is likely to have long-lasting effects throughout an individual's lifetime.

Table 3.6 Effect of abuse on development/behaviour

Area of development/behaviour	Effect of abuse
Educational attainment	+ Brain development could be affected. + Absence or lateness may affect work. + The individual might suffer from low self-esteem and an inability to focus or complete work.
Attachments and relationships	Abuse will affect an individual's ability to form attachments with others. It could cause: + anxiety + withdrawn behaviour + distrust of others + isolation.
SEND	The individual will be more vulnerable, so: + may be unable to tell others what is happening + may be unaware that they are being abused.

53

Area of development/behaviour	Effect of abuse
Physical health	+ Physical abuse and neglect may affect their physical health. + Loss of appetite may affect growth and development. + Greater risk of health conditions such as diabetes, malnutrition, poor lung function, and vision/oral health problems.
Mental health	+ All forms of abuse are likely to affect mental health and may cause long-term psychological effects. + Bullying or violence may cause extreme anxiety/loss of confidence.
Inappropriate behaviour, such as: + self-harm, suicide + alcohol and drug misuse + aggression + risky or sexualised behaviour/ promiscuity + criminality	+ Effects of abuse may cause an individual to display unwanted, dangerous or unhealthy behaviours as listed here. + The individual may try to gain adults' attention in a negative way. + The individual may try to find ways of forgetting what is happening, e.g. through alcohol and/or drugs. + The individual may carry out the same abuse on others.
Socio-economic status	+ Abuse is likely to have long-term effects on an individual's future socio-economic status – in other words, their ability to achieve their potential.

Now test yourself

TESTED

18 Why might abuse cause inappropriate behaviour in a child or young person?

19 How might abuse affect a child's or young person's ability to form attachments and relationships?

Exam-style question

4 Jamal is four and has been attending nursery for two years as the only child of a single mum. He has always been happy and settled, and has a number of friends. His mother has recently remarried and is pregnant.

Each morning, Jamal has started to become distressed when his mother leaves, and takes some time to calm down. He is withdrawn and is not interested in what is happening in the setting.

The nursery staff have asked Jamal's mother if there is any cause for his change in behaviour, but she says that she is not aware of anything.

A Give two possible causes for the change in Jamal's behaviour. [2]

B Outline what the setting might do to try to help Jamal. [4]

C What might be the effect on Jamal if nothing was done? [1]

4 Behaviour

Supporting children and young people to manage their behaviour so that they can develop friendships and respond appropriately in a range of situations is an important part of a practitioner's role.

4.1 How the stages of social, emotional and physical development may inform behaviour, and how practitioners can use this information to meet needs

Practitioners need to recognise a child's or young person's stage of development in order to support them and to prevent unwanted behaviour, but also to have realistic expectations of their behaviour. You will need to show that you understand how development links to behaviour.

Here are three examples of this.
1 Two-year-old children might have a tantrum if they cannot have what they want, because they cannot regulate their emotions.
2 An eight-year-old child might be unkind to another child because they do not fully understand the impact of their words on the other child's feelings.
3 A 14-year-old boy lacks concentration because the hormonal changes due to puberty have affected his sleep patterns.

> **Making links**
>
> Look at Element 7 which discusses patterns of social and emotional development. At what age can children/young people start to use rules in their play?

Stages of social development that may inform behaviour

REVISED

Social skills such as the understanding of social norms are developed over time. They are closely linked to emotional and language development.

> **Social norms** Behaviour shown and expected by others in any given situation.

Table 4.1 Social development that may inform behaviour

Area	Unwanted behaviour linked to development	How adults support children and young people
Understanding of social norms	Not picking up indications from others that their behaviour is inappropriate. Not understanding how their behaviour may affect others.	Coaching children and young people ahead of a new situation so that they know how to behave. Pointing out the impact of their behaviour on others.
Ability to relate to others	Difficulty sharing and behaving co-operatively. Misinterpreting other people's actions.	Playing games with babies and young children so that they can learn turn-taking and communication skills. With older children and young people, helping them to recognise other people's points of view.
Levels of empathy	Not noticing when others are upset or angry. Difficulty in seeing things from others' perspective. Saying unkind things.	Role-modelling empathetic behaviours, such as listening carefully or being sensitive to feelings. Praising older children and young people who show empathy.

55

How SEND may impact on children's and young people's social development and behaviour

The development of communication and language is closely linked to social development. Any difficulty with communication will affect how easily children and young people can connect with one another and also recognise social norms. For instance, hearing problems may lead to difficulties in communicating or language delay.

Stages of emotional development that may inform behaviour

REVISED ●

The ability to name and manage one's own emotions is linked to self-regulation. This is also linked to language development and cognitive development. Over time, children and young people learn to talk about their feelings, with young people consciously using strategies to manage their feelings, such as mindfulness.

Behaviours linked to emotional development include tantrums, frustration, anger and non-co-operation.

How adults support children and young people

Adults can use one of the following strategies:
+ Help babies and toddlers by calming them down.
+ Teach children the name of emotions and encourage them to express their feelings using words.
+ Teach children and young people strategies such as mindfulness and breathing techniques to manage emotions.
+ Encourage young people to reflect on how they can influence their own emotional state, such as listening to music or going for a run.

How SEND may impact on emotional development and behaviour

Children and young people with developmental delay may experience frustration with difficulties in expressing their emotions.

Be aware that possible reasons for developmental delay may include neglect, abuse and learning difficulties caused by chromosomal differences.

Stages of physical development that may inform behaviour

REVISED ●

Physical development is important for completing tasks independently, such as dressing or making a model. Many play activities for children and young people require physical skills.

Table 4.2 Physical development that may inform behaviour

Area	Unwanted behaviour linked to development	How adults might support children and young people
Development of gross and fine motor skills	+ Accidents caused by lack of co-ordination and skill level + Frustration as a result of not being able to do something	+ Provide activities and encouragement at all ages to develop physical skills, e.g. riding a bicycle. + Teach certain skills, e.g. how to use scissors.
Body changes as a result of puberty	+ Mood swings + Withdrawal + Tiredness + Lack of confidence	+ Provide information about the changes that are likely to happen. + Discuss feelings with them. + Encourage them to take part in exercise.

Check your understanding and progress at **www.hoddereducation.co.uk/myrevisionnotes**

How SEND may impact on physical development and behaviour

Some disabilities or learning difficulties may prevent children and young people from taking part in some activities. This can lead to frustration or isolation, so the practitioner should look for ways to create inclusive activities and remove the barriers that might prevent children and young people from joining in.

Now test yourself   TESTED ◯

1 Explain why it is important for a practitioner to understand a child's or young person's stage of development when managing their behaviour.

2 Give an example of how a practitioner may support a child or young person with social norms.

3 How might a practitioner support a child's or young person's ability to regulate their emotions?

4 Explain how puberty might affect a young person's behaviour.

4.2 How a range of individual, environmental and educational factors can positively or negatively influence behaviour

There are three types of factors which might influence children's and young people's behaviour: individual, environmental and educational.

Individual factors   REVISED ◯

Table 4.3 The effect of individual factors on children's and young people's behaviour

Individual factors that may influence behaviour	Explanation
Self-esteem	How children and young people view themselves can influence how they behave. A child or young person who sees themselves as 'sensible' or 'helpful' may find it easier to wait their turn or be patient.
SEND	A child's or young person's medical condition, learning or developmental difficulty might affect their behaviour. A child or young person who is frequently in pain might show frustration. A child or young person with an autistic spectrum condition might misinterpret what another child/young person says.
Age	As children/young people develop, they are more likely to become less impulsive and find it easier to control their emotions and impulses. This means that a two-year-old might find it hard to wait for their turn, but an older child should find it easier.

Environmental factors   REVISED ◯

These are all linked to children's and young people's experiences outside of the setting.

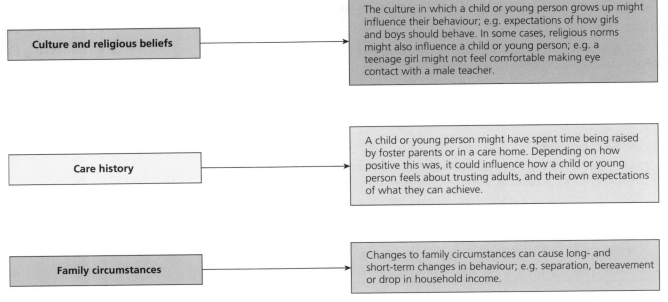

Figure 4.1 Environmental factors

Exam tip

Make sure that you also read Section 4.7 to reinforce your understanding of these factors.

Educational factors

REVISED ⬤

Three educational factors are listed in the specification that might affect a child's or young person's experience within an education setting:

✚ Bullying and discrimination – where this occurs, a child or young person can show a range of behaviours including withdrawal, anger or self-harm.

✚ Peer relationships – groups of children and young people can influence one another's behaviour in both positive and negative ways; for example, a culture of listening and wanting to learn as opposed to being disruptive. Where a child or young person does not have these friendships, they might show unwanted behaviours such as frustration, attention-seeking and withdrawal.

✚ Relationships between children/young people and practitioners – a positive relationship with a practitioner can help a child or young person show wanted behaviours such as listening and concentrating. If the relationship is poor, a child or young person might try to be disruptive or show attention-seeking behaviours.

Revision activity

Copy and complete this table. See if you can fill in the missing parts.

Type of factor	Examples
Individual	*1 Self-esteem*
Environmental	
	2 Care history
Educational	
	2 Peer relationships

Now test yourself

TESTED ○

5   Explain how age might influence behaviour.
6   Give two examples of environmental factors that can affect behaviour.
7   Explain how peer relationships may influence positive behaviour in a classroom.

Exam-style question

1   Jake has moved to a new school, following the sudden separation of his parents. He is now living with his mother, and has a close bond with her. He has not yet made any friends.

Jake has hearing difficulties, and there have been a few incidents where his hearing aids have been pulled out. His mother has explained to the school that he needs to be able to see the teacher's face; otherwise he cannot follow everything. Some of the teachers forget this and, because of embarrassment, Jake does not say anything. In a lesson today, Jake stared out of the window. When challenged, he swore at the teacher before storming out of the classroom.

Discuss to what extent Jake's behaviour might be influenced by a range of factors.

[6]

4.3 The link between self-esteem, identity and inappropriate behaviour, and the effects of over-confidence as well as low self-esteem

Self-esteem is about how a child or young person values themselves. It is linked to their identity.

Behaviours linked to positive self-esteem

REVISED ○

A child or young person who has a strong positive identity will also have good self-esteem. This makes them feel secure. They find it easier to control their behaviour, participate in activities and relate to others.

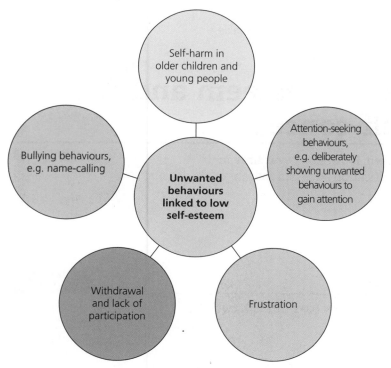

Figure 4.2 Unwanted behaviours linked to low self-esteem

59

Effects of over-confidence

Over-confidence can occur when adults constantly praise children and young people for relatively ordinary achievements while not setting appropriate boundaries on behaviour. This can lead the child or young person to believe that they are so exceptional that they need special treatment.

Children and young people who are over-confident often find it hard to make and maintain friendships with their peers.

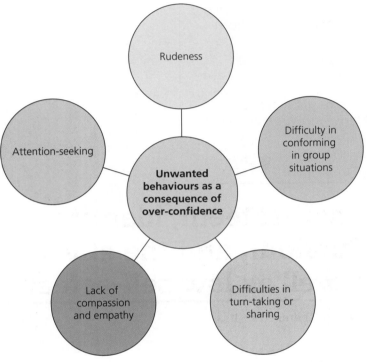

Figure 4.3 Unwanted behaviours as a consequence of over-confidence

Exam tip

Revise Section 4.4 alongside this outcome. They are closely linked.

Now test yourself

TESTED

8   Outline the positive impact of high self-esteem on a child or young person.

9   Give an example of a behaviour linked to low self-esteem.

10 Explain how over-confidence might prevent a child or young person from making friends.

4.4 How self-image, self-esteem and the ideal self inform self-concept

Self-concept is the view that you have of yourself. It develops over time in childhood and can affect behaviour. This specification suggests that there are three component parts in self-concept:

+ self-image – how you see yourself
+ self-esteem – how you value yourself
+ ideal self – how you wish you could be.

Development of self-concept

REVISED

When children/young people develop self-concept, they pass through two defining stages:

1   the existential self
2   the categorical self.

Check your understanding and progress at **www.hoddereducation.co.uk/myrevisionnotes**

The existential self	The categorical self
The child realises that they exist as an independent entity and in their own right. They can exert control on their environment, e.g. push a ball. This takes place in the first year of life.	The child begins to categorise themselves as an 'object' in the world, defining themselves in terms of age, gender, size or skills. This is a continual process. From about five years, children also gain this information about themselves by comparing themselves to others.

Figure 4.4 Characteristics of the existential self and the categorical self

The possible impact of positive and negative self-concept

REVISED ○

Table 4.4 Impacts of positive and negative self-concept

Impact on ...	Impact of positive self-concept	Impact of negative self-concept
Behaviour	Able to control emotions and show age-appropriate behaviour.	Difficulty in controlling emotions. May show attention-seeking or disruptive behaviour.
Cognition	Keen to try out new things. Show perseverance, as confident that they can gain a result. Good progress in school.	Reluctant to learn new things for fear of failure. Not motivated and lack of perseverance. Under-achievement in school.
Social and emotional development	Popular with others and able to show empathy and kindness.	Self-absorbed behaviours. Lack of confidence in making friendships.

Now test yourself
TESTED ○

11 Name the three component parts of self-concept.

12 What is meant by the term 'existential self'?

13 Explain how a positive self-concept can impact a child's or young person's development.

4.5 Why children and young people must know how to adapt behaviour to different social contexts

Adapting behaviour is about 'fitting in' and showing behaviour that is typical in any situation. You need to remember four reasons for this and be able to recognise the consequences when expected behaviour is not being shown.

Table 4.5 shows the four reasons and examples of how adapting behaviour can support learning as well as social and emotional wellbeing.

Impulse control The ability to reflect rather than act in the moment.

Table 4.5 The importance of children and young people knowing how to adapt their behaviour to different social contexts

How the child/young person can adapt	Why this is important
Focusing on learning in educational settings	The child or young person may find it easier to learn if they and others adapt their behaviour to be in a setting.
Developing **impulse control**	The child or young person might develop impulse control as a result of following the routines of the setting; e.g. tidying up equipment before getting out anything else.
Conforming to social norms	The child or young person might be accepted by others if they show the behaviour that is typical for the situation.
Making friends and maintaining relationships	A child or young person is more likely to have friends if they are able to adapt their behaviours to be 'in tune' with the behaviours that others are showing.

61

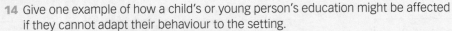

Now test yourself   TESTED ◯

14 Give one example of how a child's or young person's education might be affected if they cannot adapt their behaviour to the setting.

15 What is the link between being able to adapt one's behaviour and making friends and maintaining relationships?

16 What is meant by the term 'impulse control', and can you give an example of it?

Revision activity

For each of the four reasons in Table 4.5, can you think of a consequence if a child or young person is not able to adapt their behaviour? An example would be: exclusion from a setting and so not having the same opportunity to learn.

4.6 Why it is important to set and follow behaviour management policy and processes

Most settings have a behaviour management policy that must be followed.

This policy will set out:
+ how behaviour among children and young people will be managed
+ how staff and parents/carers coming into the setting should behave, for example, 'No smoking on premises'.

Table 4.6 gives six reasons why behaviour management policies and processes are important.

Exam tip

Remember that behaviour management policies might include how parents/carers should behave when on the premises or when contacting the setting.

Table 4.6 Why behaviour management policies and processes are important

Reason for importance of behaviour management	Explanation of reason
Input by children and young people	If children and young people feel that they have contributed to the policies and processes, they are more likely to follow the rules.
Realistic expectations	Many policies outline what is expected for different ages of children and young people. This stops adults from expecting behaviours that are not developmentally appropriate.
Fairness	Everyone knows what the policies and processes are, so there is fairness.
Safety	Some aspects of behaviour policies and procedures are about preventing accidents and incidents by putting in place safety measures.
Consistency	Children and young people need consistency between adults if they are to show appropriate behaviour. Behaviour policies and processes help adults to know how to deal with incidents and understand the expectations for behaviour in different situations.
Celebrating an individual's success	Some behaviour policies have processes so that an individual's success in learning or in showing appropriate behaviour can be celebrated, e.g. a sticker in a school assembly for progress.

Now test yourself   TESTED

17 Explain how behaviour policies can promote positive behaviours.

18 How might a setting's behaviour policy promote a consistent approach between adults?

19 Why is it important that behaviour policies and processes are age- and stage-appropriate?

Exam tip

The term 'processes' is used in this outcome, but elsewhere in this element the term 'procedures' is used. In practice, they are interchangeable.

4.7 How home, family circumstances and care history can affect behaviour

What happens out of settings is very important in children's and young people's learning, development and also behaviour. This learning outcome is divided into two sections.

+ The first is about recognising how home circumstances can affect behaviour.
+ The second part is about how this information can be used by practitioners.

Home circumstances

REVISED

Parental expectations

Parents have differing expectations of how their children should behave. This might be linked to their parenting styles. Where expectations of children's and young people's behaviour are lower than is typical for the age, children and young people might find it difficult to show age-related behaviours in settings.

> **Making links**
>
> Look at Element 5 and the section on parenting styles. Which parenting styles are linked to high expectations of behaviour?

Consistency of care

Consistency and emotional security are important in children's and young people's development. When this is not available – for example, because of family breakdown or going into care – children and young people are more likely to show attention-seeking and behaviours linked to anger and frustration.

Culture and community

The culture of the family and also the local community can impact on a child's or young person's behaviour.

+ In a culture where boys and men have more status than girls or women, a boy might not want to follow instructions from a woman.
+ In some cultures, school and education are highly prized, and so children and young people might work hard to meet the expectations of their community.
+ Some cultures and communities are more sociable than others, and children from an early age might be used to going to events and functions. This might positively affect their social skills.

Adult and child/young person relationships and interactions

The quality of attachment and the level of interactions at home can impact on children's/young people's behaviour.

+ Children and young people who have strong attachments are more likely to adapt their behaviours to social norms and also show empathetic behaviours.
+ Where relationships are weaker, children and young people are more likely to show aggression, attention-seeking and other unwanted behaviours. See also Section 4.1.

> **Exam tip**
>
> Consider what the opposite of the examples given would be; for example, a child or young person growing up in a family that rarely socialises might have lower levels of social skills.

How practitioners use this information

REVISED

The second part of this outcome is about how information about home circumstances is used to deal with unwanted behaviour. There are five principal ways to do this.

63

Table 4.7 How to use information about home circumstances to deal with unwanted behaviour

Way of dealing with unwanted behaviour	Explanation	Example
Working with parents/carers to help them find support and advice	May help parents to overcome the reason behind unwanted behaviours, e.g. lack of sleep, family conflict.	+ Health visitor referral to a sleep clinic or parenting course. + General practitioner (GP) referral to Child and Adolescent Mental Health services (CAMHS).
Sharing information with relevant colleagues to support multi-agency work and early interventions	Unwanted behaviour may be a sign of safeguarding issue, or of a development need.	+ Referral to Safeguarding Children Partnership. + Referral to an education psychologist or speech and language therapist.
Supporting individuals through planned and unplanned transitions	Transitions, especially unplanned ones, can cause anxiety and unwanted behaviour. Supporting transitions can reduce stress and help the child or young person to adjust.	+ Visiting a new setting with the child or young person. + Providing information and answering questions.
Informing a behaviour management plan Setting and tracking individual behaviour targets	A behaviour management plan sets out the strategies and targets to reduce unwanted behaviour. Understanding the home circumstances should mean that behaviour targets are realistic and strategies to promote positive behaviour are more effective.	+ Parents and other professionals talk about the child's or young person's needs, and strategies that might help them. Where possible, the child or young person is included in the discussions. + A plan is drawn up that includes targets. The plan is then reviewed and changes are made.

Making links

+ Look at Element 5. Read the section on reliable resources to support parents (Section 5.4). Can you write down two sources of support?
+ Look at Element 7. Read the section on supporting transitions (Section 7.6). List four ways in which a practitioner can support a child or young person during a transition.

Now test yourself

TESTED

20 Give one example of how culture and community might positively impact a child's or young person's behaviour.

21 Explain why supporting transitions might reduce the risk of unwanted behaviour.

22 What is the link between parental expectations and the behaviour of children and young people?

23 Give one example of a home circumstance that might positively affect a child's or young person's behaviour.

Exam tip

Remember to show in your answers that you understand the danger of stereotyping families and having lower expectations of children and young people based on their home circumstances.

4.8 How children/young people may respond to both positive and negative verbal and non-verbal communication from adults

How adults communicate with children and young people can affect their behaviour in positive or negative ways.

Non-verbal communication is often more powerful than words, especially with young children. Children and young people are quick to notice if words and body language do not correlate, for example, someone saying 'Well done' but in a bored tone of voice.

Check your understanding and progress at **www.hoddereducation.co.uk/myrevisionnotes**

Table 4.8 How children and young people respond to verbal and non-verbal communication from adults

Type of communication	Positive effects	Negative effects
Tone Sound of the voice, e.g. raised, harsh, soft or calm	Quiet, calm and slow voice tones can reduce conflict. Positive, interested upbeat tones can be motivating. Confident, warning tone may make a child or young person reflect before acting.	Angry, loud voice tones might increase conflict or anxiety. Bored tones might discourage children and young people from trying their best.
Proximity Position in relation to child or young person, e.g. standing, sitting, near or far away	Being near and at the same height as the child or young person will make the adult seem approachable. This can help conversations to flow.	Standing while the child or young person is sitting, or leaning in too close might: ✚ cause anxiety ✚ make the child or young person stand up in response. Being far away might encourage unwanted behaviour, as physical presence is reduced.
Gesture Hand movements including pointing	Positive gestures such as 'thumbs up' can facilitate communication.	Angry, stabbing movements can increase anxiety and conflict.
Body language Examples are frowning, crossed arms, relaxed positions, eye contact	Body language that seems positive and relaxed can increase communication between the adult and child/young person. Eye contact shows interest in what a child/young person is doing or saying.	Frowning, pacing or closed body language such as crossed arms can increase anxiety and conflict. Intense eye contact can seem threatening.

Revision activity

Figure 4.5 Non-verbal communication skills

Look at this picture. Make a list of non-verbal communication skills that the adult is showing. Look at the child's response. Explain whether you think that this is a positive or negative situation.

Exam tip

Remember that verbal communication is always combined with non-verbal communication – for example, frowning while talking – while non-verbal communication such as body language is sometimes the only form of communication.

Now test yourself

TESTED ⭕

24 Give an example of how tone of voice could have a negative effect on a child's or young person's response.

25 What is meant by the term 'body language'?

26 Explain how an adult's proximity to a child or young person might affect communication.

My Revision Notes: Education and Early Years T Level

4.9 How and why practitioners use positive approaches to motivate behaviour, attainment and achievement

Children and young people respond better to positive approaches. For this outcome, you will need to show that you can identify four methods that are used, give examples that are appropriate and explain the reasons for their use.

Table 4.9 Four methods to support motivation

Positive approach	Examples	Reasons
Incentive and recognition schemes	+ Marbles in a jar + Star chart + Individual stickers	Being able to receive a reward can be motivating. Can be used for groups or individual children. Rewards have to be age-appropriate and something that the child or young person wants.
Establishing and maintaining positive relationships with children/young people	+ Smiling + Showing an interest in child or young person + Being approachable	Positive attention and responses can motivate children and young people to try harder and to show expected behaviour.
Appropriate praise	'Well done! You put a lot of effort into that task.' 'I saw that you shared. That was very kind.'	Being recognised for behaviour or work can help children and young people to maintain enthusiasm and persevere. Praise works best when it is linked to the action or quality that has been shown.
Formative feedback	Comments about homework or behaviour that help a child or young person know how to make progress.	This allows a child or young person to know what they need to focus on and what is expected of them.

Making links

In Element 2, we looked at effective feedback that would help children and young people to make progress. This approach is very similar to formative feedback. How many features of effective feedback are given?

Formative feedback This provides information that will help a child or young person to make progress.

Now test yourself　　　　　　　　　　　　　TESTED ◯

27 What can incentive and recognition schemes motivate children/young people to do?

28 List two ways in which an adult could motivate a child/young person to improve their attainment.

29 What is meant by the term 'formative feedback', and how might it encourage wanted behaviour?

4.10 How and why practitioners use a range of strategies for setting clear expectations of behaviour

Clear expectations ensure that children and young people know what they can and cannot do in a situation. This can prevent inappropriate behaviour, because ground rules and boundaries have already been established. When children and young people know what is expected of them, it can help them feel more secure.

Check your understanding and progress at **www.hoddereducation.co.uk/myrevisionnotes**

For this outcome, you will need to remember different strategies for this and why they might be used.

Table 4.10 Strategies for setting clear expectations of behaviour

Strategy for setting clear expectations	Reasons for using this strategy
Establishing a structured approach	Routines are created so that children and young people know how to behave. For example: + lining up to enter the classroom + putting up their hand before talking + putting on an apron before painting + tidying away.
Acting fairly and consistently	Adults' expectations are fair and consistent with what they expect. For example: + No sitting on the table is a rule which applies to everyone.
Setting age- and stage-appropriate ground rules	Adult explains at the start of a lesson or in a new situation what children and young people can do and how they should behave.
Modelling appropriate behaviour	Adults show how to behave in line with the expectations given. For example: + They do not sit on the table or run in a corridor.
Positive reinforcement	Adults help children and young people keep to the expectations through praise and rewards, and by using positive body language.
Establishing age-appropriate boundaries	Boundaries are limits on behaviour. Children and young people are told what the limits and consequences are if they do not stay within the boundaries. Boundaries have to be age-/stage-appropriate, or children and young people will not be able to meet them.

Now test yourself   TESTED ◯

30 Explain the importance of setting clear expectations.
31 Identify two ways in which practitioners may set clear expectations.
32 How might positive reinforcement be used to maintain expectations?

Exam tip

Remember that as children and young people respond differently from one another, even within the same age or stage, a range of strategies may need to be used.

4.11 How and why practitioners use a range of strategies to support children and young people to develop self-regulation and resilience

Self-regulation is the ability to manage emotions and control impulses. It is important in being able to show age-appropriate behaviour.

Resilience is the ability to cope with setbacks, persevere and remain motivated. Children and young people who are resilient are less likely to show frustrated and disruptive behaviour because they are able to persevere and cope with setbacks.

Table 4.11 Strategies to develop self-regulation and resilience

Strategy	How it helps with developing self-regulation and resilience
Playing games/interactive sessions	Supports turn-taking and impulse control. Losing games helps children and young people learn how to 'pick themselves up'.
Sharing stories	Encourages reflection on their own and others' emotions.
Modelling coping skills	Helps children and young people to copy these strategies.

My Revision Notes: Education and Early Years T Level

Strategy	How it helps with developing self-regulation and resilience
Encouraging physical exercise	Hormones released during exercise can calm strong emotions. Can help children and young people feel more confident and so help resilience.
Encouraging problem-solving	Helps to empower children and young people and can reduce negativity.
Supporting children and young people to reframe challenges in a positive light	Can change a child's or young person's mindset and help them to become solution-focused.
Providing opportunities to support socialisation	Playing, talking and building relationships can support children and young people who have had a setback.
Encouraging mindfulness	This strategy can help with self-regulation and resilience. It can: + prevent children and young people from becoming anxious + help them to connect with their emotions.
Creating opportunities for children and young people to take supported risks	Helps children and young people to gain confidence as they try new things and learn to manage setbacks and risk.

Now test yourself TESTED ◯

33 Give two examples of ways in which adults might support self-regulation in children/young people.

34 Why are self-regulation and resilience important for positive behaviour?

35 Explain the role of physical exercise in supporting resilience.

4.12 How and why practitioners use a range of strategies to respond to behaviour

You need to be able to identify strategies that practitioners use to respond to behaviour and give reasons why they are useful. Seven strategies are given in the specification.

Exam tip

Remember that following the behaviour policy underpins the use of strategies to respond to behaviour.

Table 4.12 Strategies to respond to behaviour

Strategy	Reasons	Examples
Being fair and consistent	Helps children and young people follow the rules because the rules do not keep changing. Keeping expectations fair and age-/stage-appropriate means that children and young people do not feel that they are being picked on.	Every practitioner reminds the class to tidy up before they leave the room.
Focusing on the behaviour rather than the individual	Prevents the child or young person from developing a negative self-concept.	'It is time to be quiet' rather than 'You are noisy'.
Referring to and following the behaviour policy and student code of conduct	See also Section 4.6. Provides consistency of response by adults. Reminding children or young people about how they should behave. Can prevent children and young people from feeling that they are unfairly treated.	Practitioners deal with situations in the same way, e.g. they always tell children that they need to wait their turn on the climbing frame. 'Remember that the rule in the school is to walk when you are indoors.'
Encouraging co-regulation	Helps the child or young person to calm down and to reflect on their emotions.	Acknowledging how the child or young person is feeling. →

Check your understanding and progress at **www.hoddereducation.co.uk/myrevisionnotes**

Strategy	Reasons	Examples
Using language that clarifies expectations	Helps the child or young person to know exactly what they need to do.	'Walk now.' 'That will need to be tidied away first.'
Providing a calm and safe environment	Prevents the child or young person from feeling overwhelmed.	Creating quiet, comfy spaces for children and young people to relax.

Now test yourself   TESTED ◯

36 Explain why consistency is important in behaviour management in relation to a behaviour policy.

37 Why is it important that adults use language that clarifies expectations?

38 Explain why a calm, safe environment might help a child or young person.

Revision activity

Read through this section. Now see how many of the seven strategies you can write down from memory. Check your answers and then work on remembering any that you have missed.

Exam-style question

2 Evaluate the effectiveness of using language that clarifies expectations as a strategy to promote positive behaviour.

[6]

4.13 How and why practitioners use a range of strategies to motivate children and young people to test and stretch their skills and abilities, including setting realistic expectations

Children and young people need encouragement to stay motivated to show age-appropriate behaviour, but also to make progress in their learning. This outcome gives eight strategies that adults can use.

Exam tip

For each strategy, make sure that you can explain why it might be effective.

Table 4.13 Strategies to test and stretch skills and abilities

Strategy	Why it is used to motivate children and young people
Setting realistic expectations	Children and young people are more likely to respond to realistic expectations, provided that they are age-/stage-appropriate.
Using age- and stage-appropriate praise and encouragement	Praise and encouragement can motivate and maintain positive behaviour. If praise is not age-/stage-appropriate, it might either feel patronising or not be understood. This will reduce its effectiveness.
Involving parents/carers, as part of a whole-setting approach	Working together and having good communication can provide a consistent environment for behaviour.
Giving individuals a role/responsibility	Helps children and young people feel that others trust them and can build confidence.
Encouraging self-reflection	Teaches children and young people the skills needed to become self-aware.
Rewarding effort and success	Can motivate children and young people if the reward is appropriate. Ideally, adults should aim for children and young people to become self-motivated rather than rely on external rewards.
Celebrating mistakes as learning opportunities	Helps children and young people to be positive and move forward with their behaviour and progress.
Encouraging children and young people to recognise one another's positive behaviour	Peer support can encourage children and young people, and can create a culture of positive behaviour.

Now test yourself

TESTED ◯

39 Why is it important that praise is age-/stage-appropriate?

40 Explain why it is important to encourage children and young people to recognise one another's positive behaviour.

41 How might giving a child or young person responsibility help promote positive behaviour?

Exam-style question

3 Arti is 14 years old. She finds schoolwork hard, especially anything involving reading and writing. In lessons, she is articulate, but if a task involving writing is required, she becomes disruptive, throwing things at other pupils. The teachers often send her out of the lesson.

A new approach is being tried with Arti, in partnership with her parents. She is receiving individual tuition to support her reading and writing out of school. In school, the teachers are spending more time praising her and rewarding her success. She is also given more responsibility during lessons and when she has difficulties, she is being encouraged to ask for help more quickly.

Evaluate the effectiveness of the strategies that are being used to support Arti. [6]

Exam tip

Make sure that you suggest that a range of strategies to motivate a child or young person might be needed. This is because different children and young people might respond to different approaches.

4.14 How practitioners assess risks to their own and others' safety when dealing with challenging behaviour

Some children and young people show aggressive behaviour for a variety of reasons. For this outcome, you will need to show that you know how practitioners assess risks and prevent incidents from occurring.

Table 4.14 Assessing risks to safety when dealing with challenging behaviour

Strategy	Why it is used	Examples
Being aware of an individual's prior history	Practitioner can think about how to prevent and how to respond.	+ A two-year-old who has bitten another child. The practitioner spends more time with the two-year-old. + A 14-year-old regularly throws bookcases and cupboards over when frustrated. The practitioner constantly monitors the reaction of the young person to prevent any incidents.
Recognising triggers and early warning signs	Some behaviour has a pattern, or there are early signs that an incident is about to occur.	+ The two-year-old is more likely to bite when tired. Practitioner looks for signs of tiredness. + The 14-year-old finds writing difficult. Practitioner offers early encouragement and support.
Removing hazards and reducing risk	Removing the child or young person from a situation can keep everyone safe. Equipment might also need to be removed.	+ When the two-year-old looks tired, the practitioner does an activity just with them, away from the other children. + To prevent the 14-year-old from throwing furniture, bookcases and other large pieces of furniture are attached to the wall.
Following the setting's policies and procedures	Consistency of actions is important so that the child or young person is treated fairly and calmly. Following the setting's policies and procedures also prevents any risk of accusations of negligence or abuse.	+ As per the setting's policy, the family of the two-year-old are told in advance about how the setting will prevent a further bite from occurring, and that this will include removing the child from any potential situation. + If the 14-year-old starts to throw a chair, the practitioner knows that the procedure is to tell the other pupils to leave the room.

➜

Check your understanding and progress at **www.hoddereducation.co.uk/myrevisionnotes**

Strategy	Why it is used	Examples
Assess the likelihood of harm to self and others	Before acting, the practitioner has to think about the risk of harm to themselves and others. Acting without reflecting might make the situation worse.	+ The practitioner with the two-year-old assesses that the risk to themselves is low, but that the child might bite another child when they are tired unless precautions are taken. + The practitioner assesses that if furniture is thrown by the 14-year-old, the risk to themselves and others could be high. Close monitoring of the situation is therefore required.

Now test yourself

TESTED

42 Explain how knowing an individual's prior history might reduce the risk of an incident.

43 Give an example of why practitioners must follow their setting's policies and procedures.

44 Explain why practitioners should reflect on the likelihood of harm before taking any action.

Exam tip

Always remember to mention the importance of following the setting's policies and procedures as part of any strategy that you give; for example:
+ removing equipment in line with the setting's procedures
+ finding out about an individual's history in line with the setting.

5 Parents, families and carers

When working with children and young people, it is important to be able to work effectively with parents, families and carers. Early years and education professionals should remember the importance of effective communication and work to achieve this.

5.1 The advantages of working with parents, carers and wider families to support children and young people

All those who work with children and young people will need to be able to work with parents, carers and wider families who have responsibility for caring for them. This is because a joined-up approach will enable children and young people to achieve the best outcomes.

Remember that every time the term 'parent' or 'primary carer' is written, this includes carers and wider families.

Figure 5.1 Why is support from parents welcomed from an early age?

Table 5.1 shows some of the advantages of working in partnership with parents and valuing their support.

> **Transition** An expected or unexpected change in a child's or young person's life which can affect their behaviour or development. This includes, for example, moving to secondary school, parents divorcing or the family moving house.

Table 5.1 Advantages of working in partnership with parents

Advantage of working with parents	What this means
Creates shared expectations	The school, college or early years settings shares the same standards as parents: they will expect the same for home learning, uniform or appearance, and for babies and young children, care needs and behaviour. This consistency supports the development of the child or young person.
Makes transitions smoother	Partnership working supports children's and young people's emotional needs when making **transitions**, e.g. starting in a new setting or moving between classes.
Supports learning and development at home	Children's and young people's progress and development will be supported through positive communication and shared learning experiences.
Invites contributions from families	Good communication means that parents will be more likely to support the wider work of the school or early years setting, e.g. through volunteering or helping with events. →

Check your understanding and progress at **www.hoddereducation.co.uk/myrevisionnotes**

Advantage of working with parents	What this means
Shares information	Partnership working develops trust between parents and the setting which leads to greater understanding of each child's or young person's needs.
Supports wellbeing	Parents will be more likely to talk to staff about their child's needs or any changes which they should be aware of, so that the staff can support them more effectively.
Helps with decision-making	Sharing information, listening to others and talking things through helps when making decisions about the child or young person and their needs.

Now test yourself TESTED ⬤

1 How does sharing information with parents and carers support a child or young person?

2 Why are shared expectations between home and the setting important for a child's or young person's development?

Making links

This links to Element 7.6 around transitions. Give three examples of ways in which parents, carers and wider families can work with schools and early years settings to support transitions.

5.2 The characteristics of different family structures

Here are some descriptions of common family structures:

+ **Nuclear family**: a family unit with two parents who are co-parenting a child. This includes parents who identify as LGBT (lesbian, gay, bisexual or transgender).
+ **Single parent family**: a lone parent who is raising a child or children.
+ **Extended family**: an extended or wider family may comprise uncles, aunts and grandparents. They might all be involved in raising the child or children, along with their parents.
+ **Foster family**: foster families consist of parents who look after children who are not their own, usually for a short time.
+ **Adoptive family**: adoptive parents look after at least one child who has been adopted by them and lives with their family permanently.
+ **Blended or stepfamily**: this family unit is made up of a combination of two separate families. This means that one or both parents have children from previous relationships and now live together.

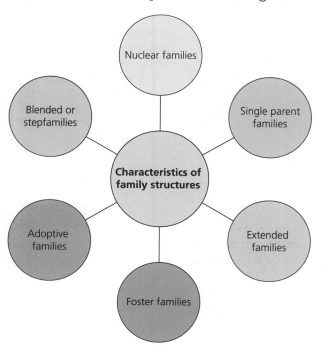

Figure 5.2 Can you identify all of these family structures?

Revision activity

Using stick people as shown, draw each type of family to help you to remember the different family structures.

Figure 5.3 Drawing the family structures might help you to remember them

Characteristics of different parenting styles

REVISED ○

Parents, carers and wider families have the greatest influence on the child or young person, with a vital role as their first educators. You might notice a range of different parenting styles.

Table 5.2 The characteristics of different parenting styles

Parenting style	Characteristics
Authoritarian	Emphasis on obedience, control and following rules without explanation. Children may not be involved in any discussion or compromise.
Permissive	Few rules or expectations. Parents are likely to have a relaxed approach and children have more freedoms.
Authoritative	Clear rules and boundaries, the reasons for which are explained to children. Parents will listen to their children and consider their views.
Instinctive	Strongly influenced by instinct or reacting to the parent's own upbringing.
Uninvolved	Lack of responsiveness; can lead to neglect.
Helicopter	A helicopter parent is heavily involved in every aspect of their child's life. This can be frustrating for the child, and in the long term will limit their independence.

Typical mistake

The words 'authoritarian' and 'authoritative' are similar, but don't confuse them as they mean different things. Try remembering that the ending 'ive' is more child-centred and putting it in a sentence. For example, 'I've got time to listen when I am authoritative.'

Exam-style question

1 Outline each of the different parenting styles, and discuss some of the possible advantages and disadvantages of each. [12]

Exam tip

Make sure you learn the characteristics of each parenting style. Even if you are not asked specifically about them, it will be helpful to understand the different types. (See the next section for why this is important.)

Why it is important to be sensitive to different parenting styles and different family contexts

REVISED ○

Educators need to be sensitive to different family contexts and parenting styles in order to work in partnership more effectively. Greater awareness also helps to:

+ value and respect families: partnership working is only possible if there is a relationship based on trust and understanding. This ensures effective communication and the exchange of information, which is vital in supporting children and young people.

Check your understanding and progress at **www.hoddereducation.co.uk/myrevisionnotes**

+ contribute to inclusion in planning and provision: being able to listen to parents and develop a relationship with them will support practitioners in planning and providing for each child's or young person's individual needs.
+ inform understanding of behavioural context: a close working partnership will enable practitioners to have a greater understanding of each child's or young person's circumstances and reasons for their behaviour.
+ inform understanding of developmental delay: parents spend the most time with their child and may be the first to notice any concerns around developmental delay.
+ inform strategies used to support behaviour and development: knowing about an individual child or young person will help practitioners when developing strategies to support their behaviour and development.
+ ensure fair and inclusive practice: this is vital to ensure that there is no form of discrimination when working with children and young people and their families.

> **Developmental delay**
> A delay in one or more areas of a child's or young person's development.

Figure 5.4 How will sensitivity to different parenting styles and structures lead to greater co-operation between families and practitioners?

Now test yourself

TESTED ⚪

3 Describe the characteristics of an extended family.
4 What is meant by a blended family?
5 Give three reasons why it is important to be sensitive to different parenting styles and family contexts.

Exam-style questions

Dilan lives with his parents and attends his local primary school. He is an only child and is in Year 5. He is able, and always completes any work which is sent home straight away.

His mother plays an active part in the PTA. You have noticed that she always takes and collects him from school, and often writes in his contact book about incidents which have happened at home or school. She seems anxious, often wants to speak to the teacher and regularly phones the school. Dilan is a quiet child who does not often put his ideas forward or speak out in class.

2 How would you identify this parenting style? [2]
3 Outline its possible effects on Dilan. [4]
4 Explain why it is important for staff who work with Dilan to be sensitive to this. [2]

> **Exam tip**
>
> Where there are several questions linked to a scenario, as in this example, make sure you read through and think about each question before you start writing.

75

5.3 Possible barriers to effective partnerships with parents, carers and wider families

In an ideal world, all practitioners and parents would have effective partnerships as everyone would like the best for the child. However, there are possible barriers which might prevent this from happening.

Table 5.3 Possible barriers to effective partnerships

Possible barrier	Explanation
Time constraints	Parents' time may be limited due to other commitments, so it might be difficult to find time for meetings or discussion.
Work commitments	Parents will have their own work commitments, which might limit their availability.
Limited resources	It might be difficult to find areas in the setting for private discussions during the day. Parents might require interpreters or need other support, such as help with travel.
Mistrust from families	In some cases, families might be wary of educators, particularly if they have not been able to develop relationships or trust with them.
English as an additional language	If English is not the parents' first language, they might find it more difficult to communicate with staff and form relationships.
SEND	If parents themselves have SEND, this might make it more difficult to form effective partnerships. Remember that: + not all disabilities are visible + parents might choose not to disclose them.
Family members' experiences	If parents have had negative educational experiences themselves, they might be reluctant to engage with the setting.

> **Revision activity**
>
> Make a list of the potential barriers. After you have learnt them, look at the ways of overcoming each one of them below, and see if you can match them together.

How to overcome possible barriers

REVISED ○

Educators need to think of ways of overcoming these possible barriers in order to support children and young people more effectively. There are a variety of different ways to do this:

+ **Having a key person:** in early years settings, each child will have a key person who should liaise with parents and build a relationship with them and their child over time. This is also a good way of starting to develop a positive relationship between home and the setting.
+ **Open door policy:** where possible, all settings should have an open door policy. This means that parents should be welcome to come in to talk about their concerns or ask questions whenever possible, without necessarily needing an appointment or set time.
+ **Encouraging home communication diaries/journals:** opportunities should be given for parents to communicate with early years practitioners and teachers using home diaries and journals on a regular basis. This is particularly important if parents are unable to come into the setting and do not have any other regular contact.
+ **Providing secure family forums:** there should be a secure online method for parents to communicate with the setting and with one another. Forums can provide information and answer concerns.
+ **Using parent/carer questionnaires:** parent/carer questionnaires can be a useful way of finding out information at specific times, such as when a child or young person starts at a setting, or if there are plans to change timetables.

Check your understanding and progress at **www.hoddereducation.co.uk/myrevisionnotes**

+ **Regular email/phone contact:** having regular email and phone contact with parents will enable the setting to communicate information on a regular basis. All settings should have up-to-date email and phone contact details of both parents, particularly if families do not live together. This is also very important in case of emergencies.

+ **Accessible buildings:** as far as possible, buildings and their layout should be inclusive and have physical adaptations, so that parents and other visitors who have different needs and/or disabilities have appropriate access to the environment.

+ **Open days/evenings:** many settings hold open days or open evenings at different times, to fit in with parents' working patterns. This enables parents to exchange information and look at their children's or young people's achievements.

+ **Translators or child advocates:** specialist support may be needed in the form of translators or sign language interpreters so that parents can be fully involved in conversations about their child. This is an important aspect of valuing each family and their home language.

+ **Home visits:** many schools and early years settings offer home visits at different stages, particularly just before young children start school or nursery. These give teachers the opportunity to meet parents and help them to feel more relaxed, as there is no pressure to travel. It also helps teachers to gain a wider picture of the child.

+ **Making use of technology:** Information can be shared with parents using social media, but also specific online platforms. These are often used in early years and give parents access and the ability to contribute to their children's records.

Figure 5.5 How do events such as open evenings support the development of positive relationships with parents?

Now test yourself TESTED ○

6 Give three potential barriers to forming effective partnerships with parents.

7 Explain why it is important for settings to have parents' up-to-date contact details.

8 What is meant by an accessible building?

9 When would a home visit typically happen?

My Revision Notes: Education and Early Years T Level

5.4 Where to find a range of reliable resources to support parents and carers and the wider family

Sometimes, parents and families need additional support if they experience difficulties in their personal circumstances or need specialist advice. Staff working in early years settings and schools need to know what is available so that they can direct parents and families.

+ Charities: charities offer support in different areas. They can often put individuals in touch with others who are in similar circumstances, and provide support with parenting skills.

+ The NHS and healthcare centres: the NHS provides support to families in a number of different ways. Although this will primarily be through physical healthcare and support, they also offer a range of children's and young people's services.

+ Community centres: these provide a meeting space for local groups such as youth clubs, uniformed organisations (Cubs and Scouts, Guides and Brownies, etc.) and sports events. They may also facilitate self-help groups which have been set up to meet local needs.

+ Citizens Advice: this organisation offers a wide range of financial and legal advice, as well as benefits which may be available to parents and families.

+ Social services: social services provide support for individuals and families and help to improve outcomes through providing guidance. They can also provide support for families by putting them in touch with specialist organisations, for example services for refugees.

+ Special Educational Needs and Disabilities Information Service (SENDAISS): provides local impartial information and support for parents and families of children who have SEND.

Revision activity

Using the following website, investigate the different charities which are available to support parents and how they can help:

www.careforthefamily. org.uk/support-for-you/ family-life/parent- support/parent-support- organisations/

Making links

Elements 4 and 6 also look at ways in which other professionals may support children and young people and their families. What other sources of support are available?

Exam-style question

5 Which **one** of the following would be a good *starting point* for advice and support for parents?
   A Citizens Advice
   B the local authority
   C a local solicitor
   D a health visitor   [1]

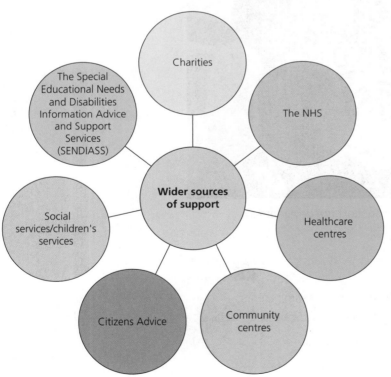

Figure 5.6 Wider sources of support

Check your understanding and progress at **www.hoddereducation.co.uk/myrevisionnotes**

6 Working with others

As well as working with parents and carers, those who work with children and young people will also come into contact with a range of other professionals. It is important to know who these may be, and understand their roles and the importance of maintaining professional relationships.

6.1 How agencies and services support children, parents/carers and wider families

You will need to have an understanding of different agencies and services in your work with children, young people and their families, and know what kind of support they offer.

Charities

REVISED

Charities may offer support to children, young people and their families in different ways depending on their needs and situation.

Charities are non-profit-making organisations and make some money from donations. They might also receive funding from the local authority to recognise the specialist support that they give.

Examples of charities that support families:
+ Family Action: transforms lives by providing practical, emotional and financial support to those who are experiencing poverty, disadvantage and social isolation across the country. www.family-action.org.uk
+ Family Rights Group: supports families by offering advice and guidance for those involved with, or needing support from, the children's welfare system. www.frg.org.uk
+ Action for Children: supports children and young people and their families in crisis, offering practical help and advice, for example, with homelessness or abusive situations. www.actionforchildren.org.uk

> **Making links**
>
> This also links to Element 5, Section 5.4. Other charities may also support the needs of children and young people and their families. Can you name some of them and the kinds of support they offer?

Figure 6.1 How might these charities support parents, carers and families?

Public services

REVISED

A public service is one which is available to everyone and which is usually considered essential for society. Examples include the police, health services and education, which are provided for free. Others include the courts and other public buildings, the fire service and social services.
+ The NHS: established in 1948 to provide healthcare for all. Services are free at the point of use (although certain services now incur a fee, and there is a prescription charge in England.)

> **Exam tip**
>
> Make sure you are aware of the kinds of public services which are free and those which are not.

79

- Children and Young People's Mental Health Services (CYPMHS): a range of services for children and young people who have mental health difficulties. Services can be offered by a range of providers. In many areas where the NHS is delivering services, children and young people will be offered help via a team known as CAMHS (Child and Adolescent Mental Health Services).
- Children's Services: provided by each local authority. They include education and social services.

Local education authorities

Local education authorities (LEAs) provide a range of children's services and educational provision as they are part of local government.
- Schools and colleges: state schools are overseen by local authorities, although the way in which they are funded may vary. Colleges are also funded in different ways, depending on their type of provision.
- SEN review team: this team is responsible for SEN assessments and reviews, and for putting in place recommendations for EHCPs for children and young people with SEND from birth to 25 years. They will take into account contributions from parents, families and the child or young person.

> **Making links**
>
> - Element 1 looks at different kinds of educational provision. When was the Education Act which raised the school leaving age to 15?
> - SEN links to Element 11. Which statutory guidance should be used when assessing the needs of children and young people with SEND?

> **Now test yourself**
>
> TESTED ●
>
> 1 What is a public service?
> 2 What is the main role of a local education authority?

6.2 The roles of other professionals in supporting children, parents/carers and families

Children, young people and their families may also receive support and guidance from professionals who are external to the school or early years setting.

Table 6.1 Roles of other professionals

Name of professional	Role
Educational psychologist	A psychologist who: - works with children and young people - carries out assessments of children's and young people's learning and development - supports parents and professionals.
GP	A qualified doctor who works in surgeries and health centres to promote the **holistic** needs of patients. They will also work with others to promote good health in the community and refer individuals for specialist treatment.
School nurse	A specialist community nurse who is usually responsible for a school or a group of schools. The role includes working with schools to promote the physical and mental health of children and young people, through duties such as: - giving immunisations - carrying out screening - raising awareness of health issues - supporting children and young people with medical needs.
Health visitor	A health professional working within the community to support babies and young children and their families. Health visitors might work in a health centre or GP surgery, but might also make home visits. →

Check your understanding and progress at **www.hoddereducation.co.uk/myrevisionnotes**

Name of professional	Role
Social worker	This professional: ✦ provides support for children, young people and their families in the community ✦ acts as advocate and guide to help improve their outcomes at challenging times ✦ works with looked after children and **vulnerable adults**, with a focus on safeguarding.
SENDCO/Area SENDCO	An area SENDCo works in several early years settings with young children who have SEND and their families. The role is to offer advice and support about additional services.
Local Authority Designated Officer (LADO)	Manages allegations against adults working with children and young people. Oversees investigations to ensure thoroughness.
Youth worker	A youth worker works directly with children and young people within the community and develops positive relationships with them. The role often includes being an advocate to support young people in decision-making.
Counsellor	Counsellors may work for the NHS or privately. They might be asked to work with children and young people who need support with their mental health and/or wellbeing.
Occupational therapist (OT)	This professional works in education and childcare settings to support children and young people with the development of everyday physical skills to promote their independence. An OT will also help parents, staff and other professionals in planning to support their needs.
Speech and language therapist (SLT/SALT)	A SLT/SALT works with children and young people to support the development of their speech or language through a range of focused strategies. They might be based in a unit in the setting, visit the setting or be based in a clinic.
Education mental health practitioner	An Education Mental Health Practitioner will work in both education and healthcare settings. Their role is to assess and support children and young people who have common mental health difficulties, such as anxiety and depression, as well as those with behavioural difficulties.

Making links

Many of these professionals will work specifically with children and young people who have SEND, which is discussed in Element 11.

Copy and complete this table to show which of these professionals are more likely to work alongside schools and which with early years settings.

Role	School/early years setting
SENDCO/Area SENDCO	
Educational psychologist	
Counsellor	
Occupational therapist	

Holistic Looking at all the interconnecting parts of something as a whole, rather than individually.

Vulnerable adult A person over 18 who needs additional care due to a physical or mental disability or illness.

Exam tip

The term 'SENDCo' is used here but you may also find this professional referred to as a 'SENCo'.

The benefits of working collaboratively with other agencies and professionals for improved outcomes

REVISED

Those who work in education and childcare settings should always, as far as possible, work collaboratively with other professionals. A consistent approach improves outcomes for children and young people for the following reasons:

✦ **Working towards shared goals**: if all professionals work towards a common purpose, they are better able to help the child or young person work towards expected outcomes.

✦ **Accessing advice and support**: a shared approach and clear communication will enable all professionals working with the child or young person to have better access to information and to share advice and support.

+ **Sharing skills, knowledge and expertise**: collaboration with others and sharing skills and knowledge helps to build up a picture of the whole child and develop better ways of supporting them.
+ **Improving referrals**: in cases where children and young people are not reaching expected developmental milestones, professionals who are working with them should collaborate to ensure that they are referred to a specialist as soon as possible.

Now test yourself   TESTED

3   Name two responsibilities of an occupational therapist.

4   What does a health visitor do?

5   How might a social worker support a child who is in care?

6   Give two benefits of collaborative working between agencies and professionals.

Exam-style question

1   Angie is working in a Reception class where the teacher would like to refer a child to the speech and language therapist (SLT) as he is not speaking at all in school and very little at home. This is affecting his ability to develop relationships with others and also to learn the phonic sounds. His mum has told Angie and the teacher that the GP is aware of his lack of speech and the referral has already been made, but she has been told it may take a while. The child has also had a hearing test but his mother says that she cannot find the results. The school SENDCo has asked her to ask the GP when the referral was made and for another copy of the hearing test results.

A   Why is it important for these professionals to work together?   [1]

B   What could happen if the child's mother does not provide the information?   [1]

C   Explain how Angie and the teacher can best support the child in the meantime.   [4]

6.3 How to work collaboratively with other agencies and professionals

We have seen that working collaboratively is in the best interests of children and young people, but it is important to highlight that this collaboration should be done in a professional way and in a way that complies with guidelines, regulations and legislation.

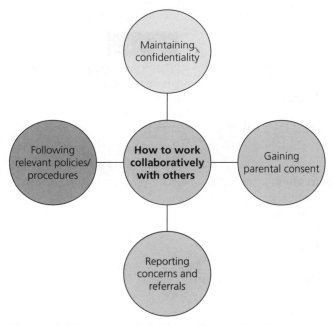

Figure 6.2 How to work collaboratively with others

Check your understanding and progress at **www.hoddereducation.co.uk/myrevisionnotes**

Maintaining confidentiality and protecting sensitive data

REVISED

Although professionals need to share information about children and young people, it is vital to maintain confidentiality. It is also a legal requirement under data protection legislation (see Unit 3) to protect sensitive data, such as personal information. Always remember that information should be given to others only on a 'need to know' basis.

Gaining parental consent when appropriate

REVISED

It is important for practitioners to obtain the consent of parents if their child will be working with other professionals. For example, they may be visited by the school nurse in Year 5 or 6 to talk about puberty. In this situation, a letter or email will be sent to parents so that they can give their consent.

Reporting concerns and referrals

REVISED

Those who work with children and young people need to consult parents and carers before reporting concerns about their child to others. This is because they have parental responsibility and should be aware of what is taking place, especially as sensitive information may be passed on.

When parental permission has been obtained, the child or young person can be referred to another professional so that their needs can be met.

Following relevant policies/procedures

REVISED

Staff should be aware of their setting's policies and procedures when working with other professionals. This is because all those working in the team will need to know in what order or according to what procedure any action will be taken.

In the context of SEND, most referrals will be made through the school or area SENDCo after parental permission has been obtained.

Making links

This relates to Element 10: Equality and diversity, around legal requirements and policies. What policies should your setting have relating to confidentiality, equality and diversity, and SEND?

Now test yourself

TESTED

7 Outline why it is important to be able to work collaboratively with other professionals when working with children and young people.

8 Why should practitioners follow policies and procedures when working with others?

9 Give an example of when an early years professional might need to work alongside other professionals.

Exam tips

+ Remember that following your setting's policies applies in all situations, not just when working with others: always mention this in your answers.
+ The use of policies and procedures will also apply to volunteers who are working in the setting.

Exam-style question

2 Paul is working in an early years setting as a volunteer and is accompanying a small group of children to visit the garden centre as part of a topic on growing. He has his phone with him and decides to take some pictures while garden centre staff are talking to the children so that he can share them with others in the setting and with parents. Paul has not been given any information about the use of his phone to take photos or about confidentiality, and only finds out that he should not have done this after he shows the photos to his manager.

   A How could this situation be avoided? [2]
   B Consider whether Paul should have done anything differently. [6]

6.4 Why practitioners establish and maintain professional boundaries and relationships with children/young people, families and other professionals

Those who work with children and young people and others need to ensure that their relationships remain within a set of professional boundaries. There are a number of reasons for this, shown in Table 6.2.

Table 6.2 The importance of professional boundaries

Benefit of professional boundaries	Explanation
Facilitates partnership working	Working within professional boundaries ensures that partnerships stay focused on their joint purpose, which is the needs of the children and young people they are supporting.
Protects emotional wellbeing	When working with children and young people, staff should as far as possible support and protect their emotional health and wellbeing. Part of remaining professional involves keeping children and young people safe, and ensuring they feel protected.
Respects privacy	Respecting the privacy of children and young people is vital for their dignity and rights, and to earn their trust. Professionals' knowledge and information about children's and young people's lives should always remain private. Practitioners may also need to help children and young people with personal care, and should treat them with respect at all times.
Avoids distraction	Retaining professional boundaries will ensure that those working with children and young people are not distracted from their role. They will understand what their role requires in different situations and what action they should take.
Provides structure and expectations	Professionalism provides structure and boundaries to the relationship between adults and children and young people, and so ensures that roles are clear.
Reduces conflict	It is important that professionals communicate well and listen to other people's views so that misunderstandings and conflict are less likely to occur.
Promotes safeguarding and prevents misuse of power	Remaining professional is important as it ensures that practitioners value individuals and retain a position of trust. This will also ensure that children and young people are kept safe.
Maintains confidentiality	Confidentiality is essential when working with children and young people, and this is an important aspect of remaining professional.

Revision activity

Learn the reasons for maintaining professional boundaries. Make a list to see how many you can remember.

How practitioners' use of social media can be detrimental

REVISED ⬤

It is very important to remember that when working with children and young people and their families, practitioners do not use social media to communicate with them. This is because it blurs the line between personal and professional relationships. As social media is unrestricted, it also means that inappropriate comments or behaviour online are not monitored by the setting and so are difficult to detect.

Most settings have a policy around the use of social media, and all staff will need to be aware of this. It is particularly detrimental to the following areas:

+ professional boundaries
+ effective partnership working
+ confidentiality
+ safeguarding.

Professional boundaries

Social media is often based around the sharing of personal information or opinions, social situations and photos. Sharing this information with children and young people and their families will reduce the ability to remain professional.

Effective partnership working

Through the use of social media, effective partnership working may be less likely – professionals could lose the trust of children and young people and their families, who will be less likely to share information.

Confidentiality

As we have seen, confidentiality is a vital part of a practitioner's work with children and young people. The use of social media would make it more difficult to remain confidential.

Safeguarding

Using social media with children and young people has serious implications for safeguarding, and it is inappropriate to use it with them. It can also put the member of staff at risk of accusations of abuse.

Figure 6.3 Why is the use of social media a potential safeguarding issue?

Now test yourself · TESTED ◯

10 How might professional boundaries reduce the likelihood of conflict with others?

11 Why is it important for professionals to respect children's and young people's privacy?

12 Name three reasons that the use of social media is detrimental to professional relationships.

Exam-style question

3 Roz is working in a secondary school and supports pupils in the Modern Languages department. At present the school has some exchange students visiting from Germany and when she arrives home one night, Roz finds that three of the students have sent her friend requests on social media.

Explain the steps Roz should take in this situation and discuss why they are important.

[6]

7 Child development

Understanding how children grow and develop is important. It helps practitioners to plan resources and activities, and also to identify when children may need additional support.

7.1 The expected patterns of development in infancy, early childhood, middle childhood and adolescence

For this outcome, you will need to spend time learning the typical patterns of development.

Cognitive development

REVISED ●

This means developing the skills that are linked to thinking. These include information processing, which is about the way information is taken in using our senses (sensory processing) and stored in our memories. The ability to remember or retrieve information is linked to this process.

Significant changes in the brain structure as a result of life experiences and maturing mean that older children and adolescents can use abstract concepts such as number and think increasingly more logically.

Table 7.1 Skills linked to cognitive development

Age range	Typical cognitive skills developed at this age
0–12 months	+ able to focus on objects up to 1 foot (approx. 30 cm) away + becoming aware of physical sensations such as hunger and thirst + increasing interest in the environment and plays with objects + from 8 months, looks for an object that has been seen and then hidden in front of them (object permanence)
1–2 years	+ understanding and responding to simple instructions from others + able to identify familiar objects in books + able to remember and repeat past events
2–3 years	+ can categorise objects + can name familiar objects in books + able to sort blocks from the smallest to largest
3–5 years	+ able to organise objects by size, shape and colour + increasingly curious and asks questions to gather information + understands the concept of past and present
5–7 years	+ understanding the concepts of space, time and dimensions + can carry out simple addition and subtraction + beginning to reason and debate with others
7–11 years	+ able to read and write + able to play games with rules + can tell the time from around 8 years + can talk about hypothetical events + able to do some mental maths

Check your understanding and progress at **www.hoddereducation.co.uk/myrevisionnotes**

Age range	Typical cognitive skills developed at this age
11–16 years	+ in some situations, able to be systematic to solve problems, e.g. searching for a lost object carefully and taking time + developing the ability to predict and speculate + enjoys discussing complex issues such as whether everyone should earn the same wage + speed increases on some tasks as memory and processing skills develop, e.g. quicker to spot matching cards in games + playing games requiring strategy + able to analyse information and draw conclusions

Revision activity

Copy and complete this table: match the skills to the age ranges.

Age range	Cognitive skill
0–1 years 1–2 years 2–3 years 3–5 years 5–7 years 7–11 year 11–16 years	+ can play games requiring strategy + develops object permanence + can sort blocks from largest to smallest + understands concept of past and present + can identify familiar objects in books + can do some mental maths + can carry out simple addition

Physical development

REVISED

These are the skills that allow us to move as well as manipulate objects.
+ At first babies rely on their reflexes for movements, but during the first six months, the baby starts to learn how to control their hands, arms and feet.
+ Over the next few years, movements become increasingly co-ordinated and skilled.
+ During adolescence, strength and stamina are gained. There can be significant differences between children when skill levels increase as a result of practice.

Physical development is divided into two broad categories:
1 Gross motor skills: large movements that involve the whole body, for example, throwing, running.
2 Fine motor skills: small movements to control the body (especially the hands) more precisely, for example, threading a needle.

Table 7.2 Skills linked to physical development

Age	Fine motor movements	Gross motor movements
Birth	Babies are born with a range of survival reflexes, such as the palmar reflex where babies grasp anything that touches their palm.	
6 months	+ can reach and grasp toys	+ can roll from front to back
9 months	+ can play with simple toys, e.g. rattles, cups	+ can sit up alone
12 months	+ points to objects using index finger	+ can pull self up to standing
1–2 years	+ can build a tower using three bricks	+ walks down steps one step at a time, using two feet to each step + towards two years, can run and stop without knocking into objects
2–3 years	+ draws circles and horizontal and vertical lines	+ walks up and down steps and can jump from the lowest steps + can stand and walk on tiptoe

My Revision Notes: Education and Early Years T Level

Age	Fine motor movements	Gross motor movements
3–5 years	+ can use scissors to cut along a line	+ can balance on one foot + uses alternate feet when walking up and down steps
5–7 years	+ can colour within the lines of a picture	+ can walk backwards quickly + uses co-ordinated movements for climbing, swimming and riding a bike
7–11 years	+ drawings increasingly detailed and skilled + handwriting may be joined up	+ increased co-ordination allowing for skill in sports, e.g. football, gymnastics, swimming
11–16 years	+ Puberty may temporarily affect fluency of movements after a growth spurt. + Changes in body shape may affect spatial awareness. + During puberty, heart and lungs grow, and there is a potential for increased stamina. + Changes during puberty also increase strength as there is more muscle development.	
16+	High level of skills in both fine and gross motor development, but skill level on any task is dependent on how much time is spent on the activity. This in turn links to interest levels.	

Exam-style questions

1 Which of these is an example of a fine motor skill?
   A kicking a ball
   B drawing a picture
   C riding a tricycle
   D walking upstairs   [1]

2 Corrie's fine and gross movements are typical for his age group. He loves climbing and riding his bike. He can walk backwards. He likes colouring and can cut out a simple shape.
   A Identify Corrie's age group.   [1]
   B Explain what his next steps in physical development are likely to be.   [4]

Exam tip

Make sure that you know the difference between a fine motor skill and a gross motor skill.

Social and emotional

REVISED ●

Social and emotional development is linked to the ability to make relationships, co-operate with others and express emotions. Typical patterns of social and emotional development depend on the quality of attachment. (See Section 7.2.)

Parallel play Playing next to another child but not with them.

Table 7.3 Skills linked to social and emotional development

Age range	Typical social and emotional skills developed at this age
0–1 year	+ starts to focus on familiar faces and smile + begins to cry when play ceases + may self-soothe by sucking fingers or rocking
1–2 years	+ beginning to empathise with another person's distress by showing own distress + shows affection to familiar family members and friends + starting to experience anxiety when separated from primary carers
2–3 years	+ engaging in **parallel play** + showing kindness and compassion towards others spontaneously + showing increasing independence
3–5 years	+ starting to verbalise a range of feelings + separating from primary carers more easily + expressing likes and dislikes
5–7 years	+ beginning to feel self-conscious and embarrassed + can co-operate in deciding rules to games + able to communicate with others freely and without prompts from adults →

Age range	Typical social and emotional skills developed at this age
7–11 years	+ friendships are stable and important, usually same gender + understand rules and consequences + able to manage their immediate impulses + self-esteem is usually positive in this period
11–16 years	+ increasing amount of time is spent with friends than with family members + increasing levels of insecurity as a result of puberty, peer pressure and developing sense of the ideal self (see Element 4, page 50) + exploration of own identity and a distancing from family

Revision activity

Look at Table 7.3. Highlight or tick which of these points are descriptions of emotional development.

Now test yourself TESTED

1 Explain what is meant by fine motor movement.
2 Give an example of a child's cognitive development between three and five years.
3 How might emotional development be affected by puberty?

Exam-style question

3 Identify two ways in which the social and emotional development of a child aged two-and-a-half differs to that of a child aged nine years. [2]

7.2 The key concepts of attachment theory and how early attachments influence adult relationships

Attachment is the development of an emotional bond between a child and key adults in their lives. In this outcome, you will need to show that you understand the importance of early attachment in relation to children's later emotional development, and be able to outline the key concepts of four attachment theories.

> **Attachment** An emotional bond.

The importance of early attachment REVISED

Early attachment is important as it:
+ provides a template for socialisation, for example, friendships, adult relationships
+ creates emotional security which is important in the development of self-esteem
+ supports the development of empathy and is linked to showing caring behaviours.

Key features of attachment theory REVISED

Different theorists have built on one another's work to produce theories of attachment. You need to revise and consider the impact of the work of:
+ John Bowlby
+ Mary Ainsworth
+ Michael Rutter
+ Rudolf Schaffer and Peggy Emerson.

Table 7.4 Features and strengths of theorists' work

Theorist	Features of work	Strengths and limitations
John Bowlby	Attachment is an **innate** process. Babies form a single attachment, usually to the mother. A internal working model or template about relationships is developed which affects later relationships. Maternal deprivation, e.g. being separated from mother, can cause later emotional and behavioural difficulties.	Strengths: ✚ The first to understand the role of attachment in later emotional development. ✚ Influenced practice, e.g. mothers now allowed to stay with their child in hospital. Limitation: ✚ Later studies showed that babies developed multiple attachments.
Mary Ainsworth	Researched attachment styles using the 'Strange situation experiment' where mothers left their babies aged around 9–18 months with strangers. Observed four patterns of attachment: 1 **Secure** – mother responsive to child's needs. Where mothers were less responsive or inconsistent, three other patterns observed: 2 **insecure avoidant** 3 **insecure ambivalent** 4 **disorganised-disoriented** (also known as disorganised attachment).	Strengths: ✚ Recognised that the quality of attachment mattered. ✚ Influenced practice, e.g. support for parents to improve attachment. Limitations: ✚ Experiment was criticised for being unethical. ✚ Experiment not considered to be reliable when carried out in other cultures.
Michael Rutter	Compared the outcomes for children who had never formed an attachment (privation) and those who had formed an attachment, but had been separated (deprivation). Concluded that privation is far more detrimental than deprivation.	Strengths: ✚ Influenced practice – babies removed at birth are placed with a foster family rather than in an institution. ✚ More support for new parents to help with attachment.
Rudolf Schaffer and Peggy Emerson	Quality of attachment linked more to responsiveness of carers rather than the amount of time spent. Babies were capable of multiple attachments. Four stages of attachment were observed: 1 **Asocial stage** (0 to 6 weeks): babies prefer humans over other objects, but can be settled by anyone.	Strengths: ✚ Quality rather than quantity of time matters in attachment, reassuring working parents that their babies will not 'forget' them if they go to childcare. ✚ Shows that babies can attach to practitioners, allowing parents to return to work/ leave babies for the day.
	2 Indiscriminate attachments (6 weeks to 6 months): babies are more sociable and can tell individuals apart but do not form strong attachments; no fear of strangers. 3 Specific (7 months+): separation anxiety when their primary attachment figure leaves; a fear of strangers develops. 4 Multiple (10/11 months+): infants form multiple attachments, such as grandparents, friends, childminders/ nursery practitioners.	✚ Has influenced when babies are taken into care.

Innate Something that occurs naturally.

Secure attachment Before separation, the child explores the environment and interacts with strangers. After separation, the child is distressed but soon calms down when mother appears.

Insecure avoidant Before and during separation, little exploration. During separation, the baby does not react when the parent leaves or returns.

Insecure ambivalent Before and after separation, the child is clingy and fearful, and shows difficult behaviours.

Disorganised-disoriented Term used when child's behaviour during separation cannot be categorised.

Asocial stage Baby is neither sociable nor unsociable.

Exam tip

Make sure that you know what the key terms used to categorise the quality of attachment are.

Check your understanding and progress at **www.hoddereducation.co.uk/myrevisionnotes**

Now test yourself   TESTED ⬤

4 Explain what the term 'multiple attachment' means.
5 Give one example of how Ainsworth's work has influenced practice.
6 What is meant by the term 'privation'?

Exam-style question

4 John Bowlby is sometimes referred to as the 'father of attachment theory'. Evaluate the influence of his work in relation to early years practice.   [6]

Revision activity

1 Write four cards with the name of the theorists on them.
2 On four other cards, write down the key points of their work.
3 Mix up the cards and see if you can match the right theorists to their work.

7.3 The differences between receptive and expressive language

This outcome is divided into two sections. The first section looks at definitions of receptive and expressive language. The second section is more complex, looking at theories of language development.

Exam tip

Allow plenty of time to look at the theories of language development. They are complex, and it is important that you clearly understand them.

Receptive and expressive language   REVISED ⬤

When children's language is being assessed, two components are considered.
1 Receptive language: the ability to comprehend or understand what is being said.
2 Expressive language: the ability to use vocabulary and form sentences to express meaning.

Babies understand (receptive language) before being able to talk (expressive language). Both components are important, and a delay in either one can affect social, emotional and cognitive development.

Making links

Read Section 7.1. Look at patterns of language development in babies and young children. From what age are most babies starting to say one or two words?

Theories in relation to children's/young people's language development   REVISED ⬤

For this outcome, you need to be able to understand the key concepts of five theorists.

Exam tip

Piaget, Vygotsky, Bruner and Skinner were included in Element 2, but the focus was different. Make sure that you are confident about their work in relation to language.

Table 7.5 Theories in relation to language development

Theorist	Key concepts	Strengths and limitations
Noam Chomsky	Language is an innate skill. Children are born with the ability to detect grammar and to make sense of the sounds of a language. He used the term '**Language Acquisition Device (LAD)**' to explain this ability.	Strength: ✦ Explains the way that children develop language. Limitation: ✦ Does not focus on the role of the adult which is recognised as essential. ➜

91

Theorist	Key concepts	Strengths and limitations
Jean Piaget	Children's thinking develops over time and language was a tool to support thought. He used the term '**schema**' to explain patterns or conclusions as a result of the thinking process. His complex theory of cognitive development has four stages (see below).	Strength: + Explains why young children talk to themselves (egocentric speech). Limitation: + He underestimated young children's ability to think logically.
Jerome Bruner	Adults instinctively know how to support children's language, e.g. by simplifying and scaffolding. He used the term '**Language Acquisition Support System (LASS)**' to describe this.	Strength: + Explains the way in which adults universally talk differently to babies than to adults.
Lev Vygotsky	Viewed language as central to learning. Children learn to use language to think. Language and logical thinking is developed through interactions.	Strength: + Explains why children who have quality interactions with adults may develop better thinking skills (see also metacognition, page 34).
BF Skinner	Behaviourist model of language. Children develop language through external stimuli rather than it being an innate process, e.g. + Adult smiles when baby babbles. + Baby babbles more as he has been positively reinforced by the smile of the adult.	Limitation: + Does not explain the way in which language develops, and how grammar develops in a similar way regardless of where children are.

Jean Piaget's stages of thinking

As part of this outcome you will need to learn the four stages that Piaget outlined.

Table 7.6 Piaget's four stages of language development

Stage	Explanation
Sensorimotor	Language use is egocentric. Crying is to meet babies' own needs.
Pre-operational	Children continue to use egocentric language. They may talk as they play. One feature of this stage is 'animism'. Their use of language reflects this, e.g. giving a cuddly toy a voice. In this period, children start to use language symbolically and talk about things that are not present.
Concrete operations Formal operations	Children's language changes in line with their ability to think logically. In this period, they use 'socialised' language reflecting their ability to 'decentre' – recognising that others may have different perspectives.

Now test yourself	TESTED ⦿

7   What is meant by the term 'egocentric speech' in relation to Piaget's theory?

7.4 How practitioners, parents, carers and other professionals can promote language development at different ages

There are many ways in which practitioners can support language. Some of these will depend on the age and stage of a child or young person. Five age groups are listed in the specification.

Strategies to promote language from birth to two years

In this phase, babies and toddlers need to link individual words and phrases to meanings. They also are developing the skills of communication, such as smiling or making eye contact.

Practitioners can use six strategies, as shown in Figure 7.1.

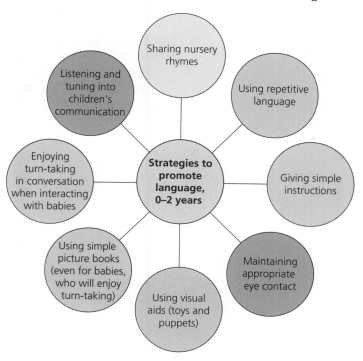

Figure 7.1 Strategies to promote language from birth to two years

Strategies to promote language from two to four years

In this phase, children need plenty of adult interaction to develop their language skills. You need to learn four strategies to promote language for this age group: see Figure 7.2.

Figure 7.2 Strategies to promote language from two to four years

Strategies to promote language from four to seven years

REVISED

In this phase, children need to develop their vocabulary and ways of using language. Four strategies to promote language are given: see Figure 7.3.

Paired reading Where a child and an adult or a more fluent child reader share a book together.

Revision activity

Can you give an example of a word game that can be used with a six-year-old?

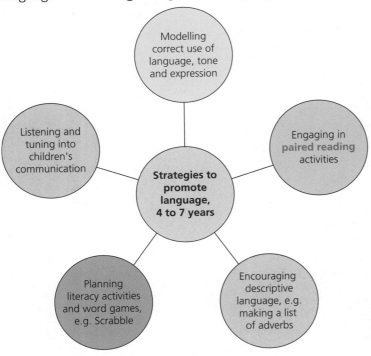

Figure 7.3 Strategies to promote language from four to seven years

Strategies to promote language from 7 to 11 years

REVISED

In this phase, the focus is increasingly on literacy activities as well as helping children to use language for thinking. Four strategies are given: see Figure 7.4.

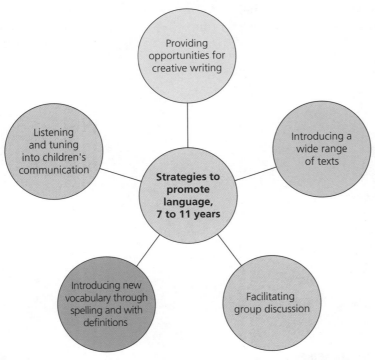

Figure 7.4 Strategies to promote language from seven to eleven years

Check your understanding and progress at **www.hoddereducation.co.uk/myrevisionnotes**

Strategies to promote language from 11 to 19 years

In this phase, young people need to become confident using language to persuade, communicate and develop further their vocabulary. Four strategies are given for this age range: see Figure 7.5.

Figure 7.5 Strategies to promote language from eleven to nineteen years

Now test yourself   TESTED ○

8   Explain how books can be used to promote language at different ages.

9   Give one example of a strategy that can promote a baby's language.

10 Identify two ways in which a 14-year-old's vocabulary can be developed.

Revision activity

For each age group, identify the role of books or reading.

7.5 How children and young people develop friendships from infancy through to adolescence

This is a long outcome and can be divided into three sections for the purposes of revision:

1   Robert Selman's framework
2   Henri Tajfel's and John Turner's social identity theory
3   positive impact of friendships.

Robert Selman's five-level framework for understanding developmental trends in children's friendships

Selman suggested that how friendships worked depended on the age and stage of the child or young person. He outlined five stages, as shown in Table 7.7.

Table 7.7 Selman's five-level framework

Level	Stage	Age when this appears	Features of this stage
Level 0	Momentary physical interaction	3–6 years	Friendship may be fleeting. Friendship is driven by circumstance, e.g. both playing in the sandpit.
Level 1	One-way assistance	5–9 years	No understanding of the reciprocal nature of friendship, e.g. being kind to each other.
Level 2	Two-way fair weather co-operation	7–12 years	Friendship may end if one child feels that they are not getting anything in return.
Level 3	Intimate, mutual sharing	8–15 years	Acts of kindness and generosity occur without an expectation of a reciprocal action.
Level 4	Mature friendship	12 years+	Ability to accept others and be accepted. Understanding that their friends will also have other, different friends.

Exam tip

Milestones for social development do not necessarily tally with Selman's theory. If you write about friendship in relation to a child's age, make sure that you use phrases such as 'according to Selman' to show that you understand this.

Revision activity

Make five cards. On each card write down the name of a stage from Selman's stages of friendship. Mix them up and see if you can order them, Level 0–4.

Key concepts of Henri Tajfel's and John Turner's social identity theory

REVISED

This theory focuses on why as children become older, they form groups with distinct identities, such as 'nerds' or 'popular kids'. The theory applies to older children and young people.

Why do older children and young people form groups?

Being in a group is linked to forming a social identity; for example, who am I when I am with a lot of people, and where do I fit in?

'In-groups' and 'out-groups'

Henri Tajfel and John Turner used the terms 'in-group' (us) and 'out-group' (them). The in-group is the one that a child or young person is part of. The out-group refers to the other group or groups that are seen as rivals or inferior.

The three stages of social identity

A child's or young person's social identity develops in three stages:

1 Categorisation: recognising the characteristics of different groups and linking these to own characteristics. For example, 'This group is good at music. I am also good at music.'

2 Identification: once a child or young person is part of a group, the actions and thoughts of the child or young person reflect those of the group. As other members of the group are also modifying their behaviours to fit in, the group identity becomes stronger.

3 Comparison: the group and the individuals within it increasingly compare themselves to other groups in order to feel superior. This maintains their self-esteem.

Table 7.8 shows positive and negative impacts of group identity.

Table 7.8 Impacts of group identity

Positive impacts of group identity	Negative impacts of group identity
There is: + a strong sense of self-concept and confidence + a feeling of protection and belonging + a sense of purpose.	+ Group behaviour can become extreme – bullying and discriminatory behaviour. + Individuals who are not part of any group can feel isolated. + Group behaviour that affects attitudes towards learning can negatively impact on progress.

Exam-style question

5 Pablo is 14 years old. He has moved to a new school. In lessons and in the playground, he is finding it hard to fit in and make friends.

In one lesson, Pablo challenges something that the teacher says. A few pupils laugh and afterwards start talking to him. Pablo begins to be accepted by this small group. The group's ethos is to test the boundaries of the school. They deliberately wear their uniform in ways that will attract attention. In lessons, they rival one another to see how many times they can stop the teacher from teaching.

At first, Pablo does not join in often. However, after five or six weeks, Pablo is firmly established within the group and begins to display the same behaviour as the rest of the group. His parents are called to the school. They tell the school that, at his previous schools, he had always been a keen student getting good grades.

Discuss Pablo's actions with reference to social identity theory.

[6]

The positive impact of friendships

REVISED

You need to be able to explain the positive effects of friendships on a child or young person. These feature in the following areas:
+ Mental health: being with others can support wellbeing and prevent isolation.
+ Resilience: it is easy to overcome problems when friends can support and advise.
+ Social skills: having friends requires developing and practising social skills such as taking turns and listening.
+ Children and young people with SEND: friendship with others who have similar needs can be a great support as they understand feelings and issues. Friendships with others can support positive self-concept and esteem.
+ Self-concept, self-esteem/confidence: being liked and valued by others can promote a positive self-concept which in turns leads to higher-level self-esteem and confidence.

Revision activity

Create a spider diagram that shows the ways in which friendship can have a positive impact on a child or young person.

Now test yourself

TESTED

11 List the five stages of Robert Selman's framework.
12 Explain what is meant by the term 'in-group'.
13 Identify three positive impacts of friendships on children and young people.

7.6 The difference between expected and unexpected transitions, and how these may affect children in positive or negative ways

Transitions are changes that take place in children's and young people's lives. You will need to be able to give examples of expected transitions that can be planned for, but also unexpected ones. You will also need to know how practitioners can support children and young people.

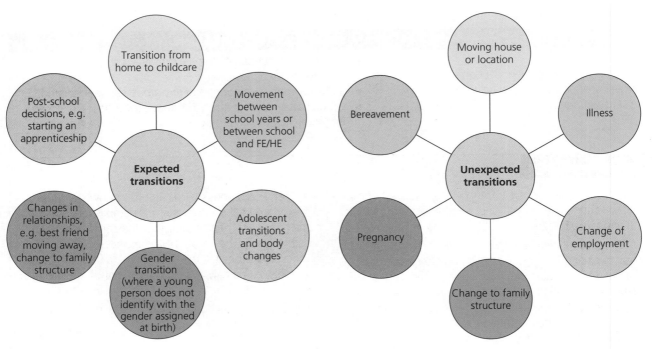

Figure 7.6 Expected transitions

Figure 7.7 Unexpected transitions

Positive and negative effects of transition

REVISED

How a transition affects a child or young person can vary depending on their age, the level of support received and the type of transition.

Examples of positive effects include:
+ the opportunity to meet new people – such as changing school or home
+ the opportunity to develop new skills or try new activities – such as starting in a childcare setting, going to college
+ increased confidence in own ability to be resilient – such as coping with pregnancy.

Examples of negative effects may include:
+ anxiety and loss of confidence
+ missing out on a relationship, for example, not seeing a parent who has moved out, moving away from friends
+ anger and/or sadness
+ jealousy, for example, birth of sibling or seeing absent parent with another family.

Revision activity

+ Make a list of as many unexpected transitions as you can.
+ Next to each unexpected transition, give an example of a negative effect.

Exam-style question

6 Which of these would be an example of an unplanned transition?
   A starting swimming lessons
   B death of a parent
   C going on holiday
   D starting school

[1]

How practitioners use a range of strategies to prepare and support children/young people through transitions

REVISED ◯

Table 7.9 Strategies to prepare and support children/young people through transitions

Strategy	Reason
Providing accurate and current information to the child or young person	Being accurately informed can reduce anxiety, as child or young person knows what to expect and when.
Giving opportunities to discuss feelings and ask questions	Opportunities to find out more or talk about feelings can help children and young people to understand the transition and deal with it more positively.
Involving individuals in their own transition planning	Having some responsibility and control is empowering and reduces anxiety.
Using **school-readiness strategies** (for children due to start Reception class)	Young children who have the skills to cope with school, e.g. following instructions and being part of a group, are more likely to cope well.
Following settling-in policies and procedures, e.g. taster sessions, visits	Provides consistency of approach between practitioners and reduces likelihood of children or young people becoming anxious.
Implementing support through a buddy system, counsellor, mentor or learning support assistant (middle childhood and young people)	Peer and other support is more likely to meet individual needs. Older children and young people may talk more to someone they have a relationship with.
Liaising with parents/carers and other professionals	Important to make sure that information given to the child or young person is accurate and consistent.
Referring individuals for specialist support as appropriate	Specialist support is needed when a child's or young person's anxiety or behaviour is complex. Early specialist support may reduce risk of self-harm or exclusion from a school or setting.

Exam tip

When answering case study type or short-answer questions, explain the reason behind your choice of strategy.

School-readiness strategies The skills children need to cope with the start of school.

Now test yourself

TESTED ◯

14 Give an example of one expected transition and one unexpected transition.

15 Why is it important for practitioners to answer children's and young people's questions about transitions?

16 Describe two strategies that might support a child or young person during an unexpected transition.

Exam-style question

7 Kareem is 15 years old. His father has lost his job and the family can no longer afford the rent. To avoid eviction, they are moving in with his aunt and her family. Kareem has been told that he will need to start at a new school.

A Identify the transitions that are taking place in Kareem's life. [3]

B Discuss potential strategies that might be used to support Kareem with these transitions. [6]

99

8 Observation and assessment

Part of the role of an early years or teaching assistant will be to carry out observations and assessments of children and young people. You will need to know the reason why this is completed at different stages in the educational process, and what you may be required to do.

8.1 The purpose of national assessments and benchmarks

Reception classes and schools are required to carry out some statutory standardised assessments. This means that the results will be checked against a standard, for consistency. In addition, students taking some qualifications such as T levels or A levels will sit exams or external assessments.

Monitoring and recording children's and young people's achievement

REVISED

National assessments and benchmarks help practitioners to:
+ monitor and record the achievements of children and young people at different stages, and to feed this back to parents and the local authority
+ look at and compare progress in different parts of the country and to feed this back to the government to build a national picture of achievement.

> **Benchmark** A point of reference for checking standards.

Differentiating between individuals' performance

REVISED

National assessments also help practitioners to look at the progress of individual pupils over time, as this will vary between different children and young people. It is also important to regularly check on their progress to make sure that their individual needs are being met.

Figure 8.1 Why might an educational setting carry out national assessments?

Check your understanding and progress at **www.hoddereducation.co.uk/myrevisionnotes**

Promoting standards and confidence in the National Curriculum

REVISED ●

National assessments take place at specific points for children and young people, starting with the RBA and Statutory Assessment Tests (SATS) in primary schools. National assessments enable practitioners to check that children and young people are working towards a similar level in key subjects. This is a way of ensuring that standards and confidence are promoted and a national picture of progress is created.

Supporting the regulation of state-funded education provision

REVISED ●

Any educational setting which is funded by the taxpayer must be held accountable for the way in which it works and be seen to give value for money. It should also be registered with and inspected by Ofsted so that standards can be checked.

> **Accountable** Required to justify actions or decisions.

> **Making links**
>
> Element 2 also looks at formal assessments within the education system. What summative assessment methods are used at the end of KS2 and KS4?

> **Now test yourself**
> TESTED ●
>
> 1 Outline what is meant by a benchmark.
> 2 Describe two of the purposes of national assessments.
> 3 Explain how Ofsted supports the regulation of state-funded educational provision.

8.2 The different purposes of formative and summative assessment

The two main types of assessment which you will need to know about are known as formative and summative assessment. These have different purposes.

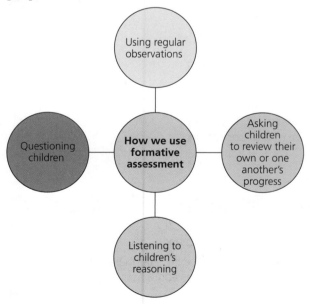

Figure 8.2 Can you think of the kind of activities children and young people might be working on when you use formative assessment?

101

Formative assessment

This is sometimes known as ongoing assessment.

It is used:
+ when practitioners are working with children and young people, to find out what they are learning
+ at the start of an activity, to consolidate previous learning or see what students can remember.

Formative assessment is carried out through talking to and questioning children and young people, observing them and listening to how they respond to different activities. This information will then help practitioners to plan for children's and young people's future learning and to set ongoing targets.

Summative assessment

Summative assessment is a summing up of what children and young people know and can do. In schools, it is often at the end of a topic, key stage or academic year. In early years, it is used to check on development at regular intervals.

Summative assessment is used to:
+ identify children's and young people's overall level at a particular time
+ provide information to parents, managers, other professionals and local authority.

> **Exam tip**
>
> To help you remember the word summative, think of summing up, or providing a summary.

> **Now test yourself**
>
> 4 Outline a type of formative assessment and describe when you would use it.
>
> TESTED

> **Exam-style question**
>
> 1 You are working in Year 6 with Harry, who is about to take his Year 6 SATS.
>   A Identify what form of assessment this is. [1]
>   B Describe other methods that can be used to assess Harry's current level. [4]

8.3 The purpose of accurately observing, recording and reporting on participation, conceptual understanding and progress

As part of the education process, practitioners make observations and assessments of children and young people in both formal and informal ways. The main reasons for observing them are to:
+ identify the progress they are making with their learning and development
+ plan for next steps.

Informally, as practitioners work with children and young people and get to know them, they will notice things about their approach to learning. This may or may not be written down. However, information from a formal observation will be recorded for a number of reasons (see Table 8.1).

Table 8.1 Reasons for formal observation

Reason for formal observation	What this means
Identifying developmental progress	Observations help practitioners to identify and track the progress children and young people are making with their learning and development.
Informing feedback for children's/ young people's next steps	Observing children and young people and using specific information enables practitioners to feed back to them and to colleagues about how they have responded to a learning activity. →

Reason for formal observation	What this means
Informing planning	Knowing exactly how children and young people are progressing will help a practitioner to work more closely with them and plan towards their next steps.
Adhering to policies	Any observations which are carried out should be in line with the setting's assessment, recording and reporting policy. They should be recorded in the appropriate way and stored confidentially, whether locked in a filing cabinet or digitally password-protected.
Maintaining validity/reliability	Observers should ensure that any observations of children and young people which are made are valid and reliable. This means that they should record only what is necessary for the purpose of the observation, and ensure that what is written is relevant.
Enabling interventions	Up-to-date observations will help practitioners to gather evidence about a child's or young person's current level of learning so that they can plan appropriate interventions if needed.
Sharing information with colleagues, the family and others	Observations will help practitioners to build up a picture of the child or young person and gather specific information to share with others, such as colleagues, parents and other agencies.

The type of recording practitioners use will vary depending on the purpose and situation:

+ Free description: a detailed description of what the child or young person is doing within a short time period.
+ Time sample: a record of how often a child or young person carries out a particular behaviour or activity within a given time period.
+ Checklist: ticking what the child or young person is able to do against a list.
+ Snapshot: a photo or brief description to capture something that the child has done. These are often used in early years settings.

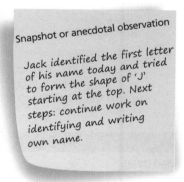

Snapshot or anecdotal observation

Jack identified the first letter of his name today and tried to form the shape of 'J' starting at the top. Next steps: continue work on identifying and writing own name.

Figure 8.3 When might practitioners use a snapshot observation?

Now test yourself
TESTED

5 Give three reasons practitioners might carry out an observation on a child or young person.

6 Why is it important that practitioners adhere to policies and procedures when recording information?

7 Explain how observations help practitioners to support the learning and development of children and young people.

Exam-style question

2 Abby has been asked to carry out a time sample observation on Jasmine, who is in a Year 2 class. Jasmine is displaying some challenging behaviour, and the teacher would like some evidence to show how regularly this happens during the day and whether there are any triggers. She has not provided a pro forma for Abby to use, but just asks for the information.

Abby observes Jasmine throughout the day and presents the teacher with several pages of information, which is more than is needed.

A Explain how the information in this observation could have been kept more valid and reliable. [1]

B Will the teacher still be able to use it? [1]

C Describe what Abby and the teacher could do next time to improve the quality of the observation. [1]

8.4 Different roles that practitioners play in assessment processes and requirements

At each different stage during the educational process, practitioners will play different roles regarding assessment.

Early years practitioners

Early years practitioners work in early years settings or in school nurseries and Reception classes.

Observe, record and review children's progress

Early years practitioners get to know their key children through observing and talking to them and to their parents or carers. They will:
+ observe the children carrying out different learning activities
+ record and review their progress by taking photos and noting down their observations.

Assess children's individual needs

While they are looking at individual children in each of the seven areas of learning and development, early years practitioners will assess their individual needs against the expected level for their age.

Plan activities and support statutory assessments

Following their assessments, early years practitioners will use this information to plan their next steps for learning.

They will also support three statutory assessments:
1 the two-year progress check
2 the RBA
3 the EYFS Profile.

> **RBA (Reception Baseline Assessment)** Assessment that is carried out at the start of a child's Reception year in school.
>
> **EYFS Profile** Assessment carried out in school at the end of the Reception year.

Table 8.2 The three statutory assessments

Statutory progress check	Description
Two-year check	A check which takes place between the ages of two and three.
	Its purpose is to provide parents or carers with a summary of their child's development in the three prime areas:
	1 communication and language
	2 physical development
	3 personal, social and emotional development.
	It also gives practitioners and parents an opportunity to identify any developmental needs so that additional support can be given to the child at an early stage.
RBA	The RBA takes place during the first six weeks that a child is in school. It is carried out by school staff, usually the class teacher.
	There is no written test, but teachers will talk to children and carry out practical tasks to assess their competence in mathematics, literacy, communication and language.
	It gives schools baseline data from which they can monitor children's progress up to the SATS in Year 6.
EYFS Profile	For each of the Early Learning Goals, teachers report whether a child is showing 'Expected' development or whether development is still 'Emerging'.

Exam-style question

3 Frankie works in a nursery. She has 12 key children and is keen to make sure that she is getting to know them so that she can build up a picture of each child. She has been asked to carry out this part of the two-year check on three of her key children and to gather information from parents.

   A Describe what type of assessment or observations Frankie might use to fill in the key person part of the form. [2]

   B Explain how carrying out this assessment alongside parents and other professionals helps practitioners to build up a picture of each child. [4]

Figure 8.4 shows an example pro forma to be filled in at the two-year check.

Prime areas of learning My strengths; where I am now; what I can do by myself again and again		
Communication and language	**Physical**	**Personal, social and emotional**
What my parents/carers think:	What my parents/carers think:	What my parents/carers think:
What my key person thinks:	What my key person thinks:	What my key person thinks:
What I like doing:	What I like doing:	What I like doing:
Is there anything we are concerned about?	Is there anything we are concerned about?	Is there anything we are concerned about?

Any other information: Share the views of other practitioners and, where relevant, other professionals working with the child:

Figure 8.4 Example of a pro forma

Source: https://www.salford.gov.uk/media/389975/progress-check-proforma.pdf

Teachers/lecturers/teaching assistants   REVISED ◯

Teachers, lecturers and teaching assistants work in schools and colleges.

Monitor children's and young people's understanding and progress

As children and young people move through the school or college system, teachers, lecturers and assistants will monitor their knowledge and understanding through different methods of assessment.

+ Each organisation is likely to have its own ongoing assessment procedures, as well as the statutory summative assessments.
+ Head teachers will usually meet teachers regularly to discuss children's and young people's progress and to identify any issues.

Provide targeted feedback to enable children and young people to improve

These professionals will:

+ give students specific feedback through their ongoing assessments
+ identify those areas which need development
+ support students in achieving their targets.

Prepare children and young people for national assessments

At the appropriate stages, children and young people will be prepared for national assessments by covering the requirements of the curriculum.

Exam-style question

4 You are working in a Year 4 class and have been asked to look at pupils' progress towards their literacy and numeracy targets with them before parents' evening. The children's targets are kept glued inside their exercise books.

Evaluate how this activity might help pupils. [6]

Assessors

REVISED ⬤

Assessors usually work with older students in colleges and sixth forms.

Assess individuals' performance/relevant knowledge

Assessors will look at the way in which students carry out their duties in the workplace. They may also question them to check their understanding about aspects of their role, or set assignments to check their knowledge.

Qualifications may vary in the types of evidence which they accept in different areas.

Figure 8.5 How do work-based observations of students support their learning and progress?

Ensure that the standards and requirements of the specification are met

Assessors will need to ensure that the student has met the standards of their qualification by looking at their competence in each area. This will include different aspects of their work such as working with others or health and safety in the workplace.

If students do not meet the standards, they will need to be reassessed at a later date.

Coaches/mentors

REVISED ○

Coaches and mentors work with older students. Their roles are slightly different, but they will:
+ offer advice and guidance
+ support students' learning and development.

A mentor may provide more long-term, informal advice and act as a role model, whereas a coach is more likely to focus on individual goals.

Set and review key performance indicators

Performance indicators will show whether a student's performance is on target. Coaches and mentors will look at these alongside students, and support them in identifying what they need to do next.

Provide support relevant to individual needs, such as special exam considerations

Coaches and mentors will get to know students so that they can identify any barriers to achievement. They will have time to listen to them and arrange for additional support where needed, for example, in exams.

Advise on how to improve individual performance

Coaches and mentors will:
+ provide guidance as part of the process
+ help students with any individual targets
+ advise them on how they can improve.

Now test yourself TESTED ○

8 What role might a teaching assistant play in the assessment process?

9 How might an assessor assess an individual's performance and knowledge?

10 How do the roles of coach and mentor differ?

Exam-style question

5 Errison has been working as a teaching assistant for a year and has been encouraged by his school to gain his Level 2 qualification in Supporting Teaching and Learning. He has enrolled with his local college and his assessor will be coming to the school to observe his practice.

  A Explain how this process will support Errison in his professional development. [4]

  B Identify two ways in which his assessor could decide how he is meeting the criteria for the qualification. [2]

9 Reflective practice

When we talk about reflective practice, we mean the ability to think about our actions and gain a better understanding of what we do. The idea is that we can then reflect upon how we can improve, i.e. use this understanding to do it better.

9.1 Key concepts of specific models of reflection

Models of reflection help with this. For this specification, you need to understand three different models:
1   Kolb's experiential learning cycle
2   Gibbs' reflective cycle
3   Boud, Keogh and Walker's model.

Kolb's experiential learning cycle: four stages of learning from experience

REVISED ●

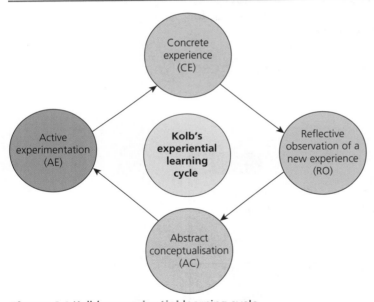

Figure 9.1 Kolb's **experiential** learning cycle

> **Experiential** Learning from experience.

Kolb believed that learners pass through all four stages, and can only learn effectively if this is the case. He also believed that although they can pass through the stages in any order, effective support from a mentor or teacher is vital so that students can be shown how to think critically at each stage.

The four stages are:
1   **Concrete experience (CE):** the learner encounters an activity or experience for themselves.
2   **Reflective observation of a new experience (RO):** the learner thinks back or reflects on their experience.
3   **Abstract conceptualisation (AC):** the learner has a new idea or has changed their thinking due to their experience.
4   **Active experimentation (AE):** the learner applies their new way of thinking to a future experience.

Check your understanding and progress at **www.hoddereducation.co.uk/myrevisionnotes**

Gibbs' reflective cycle: six stages of reflecting on experience

Gibbs' model states that learners should have six stages of reflecting on experience, which they learn and develop through repeating the process.

Table 9.1 Gibbs' reflective cycle

Stage	Process
1 Description	What happened? All details, what everyone did and the result.
2 Feelings	How did you and others feel at the time? How do you and others feel now?
3 Evaluation	What was good or bad about the situation? What were the influences on any positive or negative outcomes?
4 Analysis	What sense can you make of the situation?
5 Conclusion	What could you have done differently? What did you learn?
6 Action plan	Do you need to develop new skills? How will these help you handle the situation better in the future?

Boud, Keogh and Walker's model: three stages of reflecting on practice

REVISED

These three theorists developed the idea that there are three stages of reflecting on practice. This model has a focus on feeling and emotions, as well as on whether these are positive or negative.

1 **Experience**: What are my feelings and emotions linked to my experience?
2 **Reflective process**: As I think about my experience, how can I remove any negative feelings and re-evaluate my thinking?
3 **Outcomes**: How might my behaviour change as a result of what I have learnt through reflection?

How reflective models can be applied in practice

REVISED

Practitioners might need to use a combination of approaches when reflecting on their own learning. However, in each case, the learner needs to:
+ revisit the activity
+ think carefully about what has happened, then
+ consider how they might change or develop following the experience.

This process can help practitioners when thinking about their role, or about activities which they have carried out with children and young people.

Revision activity

To help remember the three different models of reflection, it can help to think of them alongside the number of stages. For example, Kolb's theory has four, Gibbs' has six and Boud, Keogh and Walker's model has three – the same as the number of theorists.

See if you can draw a table for each as in the example below and fill in the different stages and what they mean.

Gibbs' reflective cycle:

Stage	Process
1. Description	
2.	How did you and others feel at the time? How do you and others feel now?
3. Evaluation	
4.	What sense can you make of the situation?
5. Conclusion	
6.	

Now test yourself   TESTED ○

1   Explain why models of reflection are important to professional practice.

9.2 Current priorities and debates in education

There will always be priorities and debates around education, and it is important to know what they are so that you can keep informed of developments in theory and practice. There are a number of ways of doing this:

+ Keep up to date with the news by reading news websites and newspapers.
+ Look at educational magazines, papers and websites relating to early years or your area of education, for example.
+ Follow social media groups in a professional context to keep up to date with particular areas of interest.
+ Practise continuing professional development (CPD) (see Section 9.3) and attend additional training and professional development when it is available.

Education reform   REVISED ○

Education reform refers to the way in which education changes over time, due to new laws or government innovations. This is a continual process and some examples are listed in the specification.

The impact of National Curriculum reforms

The National Curriculum was first introduced in 1988 as part of the Education Reform Act. It prescribed in detail how 12 curriculum subjects were to be taught in England between the ages of 5 and 16.

Since then it has gradually changed, and in 2014 it was 'slimmed down'. Now only the core subjects of English, maths and science are prescribed in detail, although what pupils should be taught about in other subjects is still outlined. These reforms affect the way in which schools plan their curriculum performing subjects.

> **Core subjects** English, maths and science.
>
> **Selective education** Education in which the students have been admitted through a selection process such as a test.
>
> **Social mobility** Movement of individuals or groups between different social classes or levels.

The pros and cons of selective education

Those who are in favour of selective education (in settings such as grammar schools) say:

+ It encourages social mobility, as all children/young people from all backgrounds can take a test and get into a selective school, which might be performing better than a non-selective school.

Those who are against selective education say:

+ More affluent parents have an advantage – they can arrange tutors for their children so that they are more likely to pass the tests.
+ There are also more selective schools in some parts of the country than others, which means that the same opportunities for getting into selective schools are not available to all children/young people.

Selective education is an ongoing debate and is often discussed by governments.

High-stakes accountability via Ofsted and its effect on staff and children

Ofsted regulates and inspects educational settings and keeps them accountable, as many of them are funded through central government.

Check your understanding and progress at **www.hoddereducation.co.uk/myrevisionnotes**

This body also looks at standards in different settings and awards them one of four overall judgements about how well they are run and managed: Outstanding, Good, Requires improvement or Inadequate.

Ofsted can be the subject of criticism however. Inspections can cause stress and anxiety among staff and children in different settings.

Figure 9.2 How might Ofsted requirements affect staff and children in different settings?

How education is funded in England

The way in which different settings are funded is a topic which is often debated. Table 9.2 shows how different types of setting are funded.

Table 9.2 Education funding for different types of school

Type of setting	Funding
State or 'maintained' schools	Funded by government and run by local authorities.
	There are different types of maintained school, including community schools, foundation schools, voluntary aided or controlled schools, and special schools.
Academies and Free schools	Entirely government-funded but not run by local authorities.
	Academies and Free schools have control over their budgeting, and greater flexibility over their curriculum, finances and teachers' pay.
Independent/private schools	Paid for by fees from parents/carers.
	Receive no government or state funding, although some places may be funded by local authority if pupils are placed there for a specific reason, such as SEND.
	Some specialist independent schools may be funded through donations if they have charitable status, e.g. those run by the National Autistic Society or Royal National Institute of Blind People.

Typical mistake

Don't think that all state schools are funded in the same way. The main difference is the way in which academies are funded, as they have more control over their budgets than other state schools.

Making links

Element 1 also looks at how education is funded in England. Outline how further education and higher education are currently funded.

Now test yourself   TESTED

2   Name two current priorities or debates in education.

3   Give one reason why some people are in favour of selective education.

My Revision Notes: Education and Early Years T Level

National assessments

The arguments for and against National Curriculum tests

National Curriculum tests (often known as SATs) in core subjects have been the subject of debate since they were first introduced at different educational stages shortly after the introduction of the National Curriculum.

Although educators agree that children's learning should be measured in some way so that schools can track their progress and report to parents and the government, this can mean that they are 'taught to the test' rather than offered a broad and balanced curriculum. KS3 SATs were abolished in 2008 and KS1 SATs will be non-statutory from 2023.

The advantages and disadvantages of GCSEs versus IGCSEs

GCSEs (General Certificate of Secondary Education) are the examinations which most pupils in England will undertake at the age of 16. However, International GCSEs (sometimes known as IGCSEs) are recognised by many other countries and can be more useful for international students or for those who wish to use their qualifications in other countries, for example, if they plan to study the International Baccalaureate.

IGCSEs are not offered by state schools in England but by private and international schools. There are some differences in the coursework/exam balance and some say that IGCSEs are easier, although both are accepted by universities and considered comparable.

Exam-style question

1 Why are children required to take national assessment tests (SATs)? Choose one option.
   A Children should have regular testing.
   B Children have always been tested at 7, 11 and 16.
   C Children's progress must be reported to parents and the government.
   D SATS help teachers to have a focus at the end of a key stage. [1]

Making links

National assessments are covered in Element 8. What national assessments do children and young people sit at the end of KS2 and at age 16 in England?

Technology and education

The pros and cons of technology in classrooms

Digital technology is now an essential tool in most classrooms and can be used to enhance teaching and learning. In addition, computing is a National Curriculum subject, and in an increasingly digitally literate world, children and young people need to know how to use it.

However, there are downsides to technology:
+ It is often expensive and, due to new innovations, can become outdated quickly.
+ It can be difficult to use with groups, as technical problems with individual devices can take up teaching time for the group as a whole.
+ Schools and colleges need to have strong firewalls in place to prevent safeguarding issues, which can occur when children and young people access inappropriate sites.
+ Technology is also criticised for limiting social interactions – children and young people can be surrounded by technology in the form of phones and other devices at home.

Figure 9.3 What are the benefits of digital technology in classrooms?

The opportunities offered by blended learning

Blended learning has become familiar to many, particularly during recent periods of lockdown in the COVID-19 pandemic where it was not possible to have face-to-face teaching. Many have used it successfully and found it helpful as learning can be accessed when convenient. However, it relies on the technology working successfully and on there being enough devices available to pupils. Children and young people can become more isolated.

> **Blended learning** A style of teaching that uses a blend of online and face-to-face teaching.

Children's and young people's health and wellbeing

REVISED ●

The impact of exam stress on children's/young people's health and wellbeing

Children's and young people's mental health has become a priority in recent years as there is greater awareness of the importance of mental health in general. Emotional health and wellbeing are affected by different factors: exam stress is one factor, so adults need to be aware of signs of stress. These may include mood swings, lack of appetite or physical health problems.

The quality of support for pupils with SEND

Provision for pupils with SEND is affected by the funding which is available, and this varies between different locations. This is a regular topic for discussion and debate in the media, as, for instance, parents who understand the system may be more likely to access funding and support for their children. The quality and level of support for pupils with SEND will also affect their mental health and wellbeing as they go through the education system.

> **Making links**
>
> You will look at SEND in more detail in Element 11, Section 11.10. Name two ways in which adults can remove barriers to learning for pupils with SEND.

Now test yourself TESTED ○

4 Identify one advantage of national assessments.
5 Name two disadvantages of using digital technology in classrooms.
6 Describe how a child or young person may be affected by exam stress.

113

9.3 The importance of receiving ongoing developmental feedback

Most professionals have some form of continuing professional development (CPD). This will mean that they receive regular training and ongoing developmental discussions with their line manager or mentor, which is put in place by the setting.

> **Continuing professional development (CPD)**
> Ongoing professional training and development.

Table 9.3 The importance of feedback

Why receiving feedback is important	What this means
Improves performance	Feedback encourages you to think about your performance and how you can develop your skills.
Increases motivation	Talking to others about your role is a way of thinking about it and developing your motivation.
Enhances personal and professional growth	Feedback allows you to see your practice from another point of view. This perspective can draw your attention to different aspects of your practice.
Provides constructive criticism	The person giving feedback is often called a 'critical friend'. This means that they are there to work with you to provide positive support.
Supports reflective practice	The process of developmental feedback is designed to encourage reflection and to think about areas for development.

Why practitioners must engage in continuing professional development

REVISED

There are many good reasons for engaging in CPD:
+ **Maintain up-to-date knowledge and skills**: professional development will support practitioners in keeping their knowledge up to date, and will provide opportunities to develop different areas of their practice.
+ **Improve provision and outcomes for children and young people**: actively reflecting on your practice will improve what you are doing in the classroom and is likely to improve outcomes for children and young people.
+ **Adhere to regulatory requirements**: CPD will help you to be aware of and implement new regulatory requirements as they are introduced.
+ **Keep up to date with legislative changes**: your line manager will ensure that you are informed about any changes in the law.
+ **Ensure understanding of current priorities, debates and approaches in education**: ongoing CPD will ensure that your attention is drawn to these, and will give you opportunities to clarify anything which is unclear.
+ **Make meaningful contributions to a team**: CPD and reflective practice will encourage you to think about your own contribution to and impact on workplace teams.
+ **Improve opportunities for progression and promotion in own role**: structured CPD will give all practitioners opportunities to move forward in their role, by discussing their strengths and aspirations with line managers.

> **Now test yourself**   TESTED
>
> 7   Outline three reasons why developmental feedback is important.

> **Exam-style question**
>
> 2   Which of the following is the *main* reason why practitioners *must* engage in continuing professional development?
>   A   to have time out from the classroom
>   B   to keep up to date with current practice
>   C   to enable practitioners to look at the skills of others
>   D   to look out for additional training   [1]

Check your understanding and progress at **www.hoddereducation.co.uk/myrevisionnotes**

9.4 How practitioners can meet their own developmental needs

In addition to CPD which is enabled by others, practitioners should think regularly about their own ways of changing and improving the way they work.

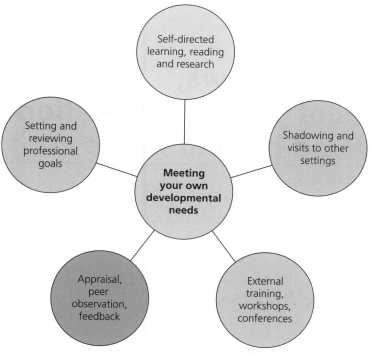

Figure 9.4 Meeting your own developmental needs

+ **Self-directed learning, reading and research**: there may be a specific area of education which interests you, or you might find a publication which is helpful to you in your role. This kind of self-directed research is one way of meeting your own developmental needs. (See also Section 9.2, Current priorities and debates in education, page 105.)
+ **Shadowing and visits to other settings**: shadowing refers to observing others in other settings who have a similar role. It enables practitioners to pick up different ideas and approaches.
+ **External training, workshops, conferences**: you may be able to ask for external training or educational workshops and conferences to enhance your practice. This kind of external training can also lead to additional qualifications.
+ **Appraisal, peer observation, feedback**: although you will set and review goals as part of your CPD, it is important to take other opportunities to observe others and ask for feedback as part of your reflection on your role.
+ **Setting and reviewing professional goals**: it is important to regularly think about and review your own professional goals so that you can look at your progress towards meeting them.

Exam-style question

3 Amir is working in a college supporting students with their literacy skills. He has been there for a year and is about to have his first appraisal with his line manager. He has been asked to fill in a form before his appraisal, which asks him to reflect on his role and think about his strengths as well as areas which may need development. This is designed to help him to set professional goals.

Choose one recognised method of reflective practice and analyse how this will help Amir to carry this out. [6]

10 Equality and diversity

This element looks at equality and diversity, and the importance of including and respecting all children and young people.

10.1 The basic principles of laws, regulations and codes of practice in relation to equality, diversity and human rights

You need to be familiar with four main areas of legislation and regulation, and their basic principles:

+ United Nations Convention on the Rights of the Child (UNCRC) 1989
+ Equality Act 2010
+ Special Educational Needs and Disability Code of Practice 2015
+ UK General Data Protection Regulation (UK GDPR).

> **Equality** Being equal in terms of status, rights and opportunities.
>
> **Diversity** The existence of differences between individuals.

United Nations Convention on the Rights of the Child (UNCRC) 1989

REVISED

UNICEF is the United Nations charity which supports children worldwide.

The UNCRC was signed and ratified by 195 countries in 1989 to protect the rights of all children and young people. The 54 articles of the UNCRC state how these rights should be met through a series of entitlements and to prevent discrimination.

Table 10.1 explains the four general principles of the UN Convention on the Rights of the Child.

> **Ratify** To vote on a written document to accept it as official.
>
> **Discrimination** Different (usually unfair) treatment of a group of people due to prejudice.

Table 10.1 The four general principles of the UNCRC

Article of UNCRC	What it means
Article 2: Non-discrimination	The UNCRC applies to every child without discrimination, whatever their ethnicity, sex, religion, language, abilities or any other status, whatever they think or say, whatever their family background.
Article 3: Best interest of the child	The best interests of the child must be a top priority in all decisions and actions that affect children.
Article 6: Right to life, survival and development	Every child has the right to life. Governments must do all they can to ensure that children survive and develop to their full potential.
Article 12: Right to be heard	Every child has the right to express their views, feelings and wishes in all matters affecting them, and to have their views considered and taken seriously. This right applies at all times, e.g. during immigration proceedings, housing decisions or the child's day-to-day home life.

Equality Act 2010

The Equality Act 2010 is the main legislation enforcing equality and respect for diversity in the UK. This means that it protects the rights of everyone and prevents people from being treated unfairly through both direct and indirect discrimination.

✛ Direct discrimination means treating someone differently from another person due to a protected characteristic (see Figure 10.1). An example might be that someone is prevented from using a venue because they have a disability.

✛ Indirect discrimination is more difficult to recognise. It means that a rule is applied to everyone but disadvantages someone with a protected characteristic. For example, if a school uniform policy states that all pupils should wear a cap without exception, this will indirectly discriminate against pupils who are Sikh, who wear a turban or topknot as part of their religion.

✛ Under the Equality Act, there are nine protected characteristics, which are shown in Figure 10.1. This means that everyone in the UK is protected from discrimination caused by these characteristics.

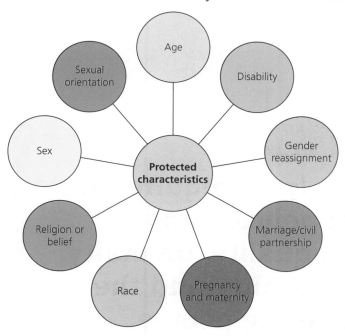

Figure 10.1 Why is it important that individuals are not discriminated against on the basis of these characteristics?

Special Educational Needs and Disability Code of Practice 2015

This Act outlines the four broad areas of need which may be experienced by a child or young person with SEND. They may be affected by one or more of these, which may be interrelated: for example, a child or young person with cognition and learning difficulties may also have problems with their speech and language.

1 Communication and interaction: difficulties in the area of speech, language and communication.

2 Cognition and learning: difficulties with different aspects of learning. These may be wide-ranging and can range from specific learning difficulties, such as dyslexia or dyscalculia, to those which are severe or profound.

> **Dyslexia** A learning difficulty which mainly affects a person's reading and writing skills.
>
> **Dyscalculia** A learning difficulty which mainly affects a person's ability to use numbers.

3 Social, emotional and mental health: the child or young person has difficulties in managing their relationships and emotions. This may also lead to mental health conditions.

4 Sensory and/or physical: a physical need such as a physical disability, or a sensory impairment which may affect their vision or hearing.

> **Typical mistake**
>
> Remember that not all disabilities are visible to others.

UK GDPR legislation

REVISED ⬤

The GDPR was originally introduced as part of EU legislation and has been adopted by the UK via the UK General Data Protection Regulation (UK GDPR).

It relates to the way in which organisations store information which they hold on individuals, including staff, children and visitors or volunteers. This may include personal information such as names and addresses, qualifications and medical records as well as records of children's and young people's progress.

> **Now test yourself**   TESTED ⬤
>
> 1 What is meant by the term 'equality'?
> 2 How would you define 'direct discrimination'?
> 3 Name four of the protected characteristics covered by the Equality Act 2010.

> **Exam-style questions**
>
> 1 Identify the four broad areas of need as defined by the SEND Code of Practice 2015. [4]
> 2 Explain how the UNCRC 'best interest of the child' principle promotes the rights of children and young people. [4]

10.2 The links between legal requirements and the organisational policies and procedures relating to equality, diversity, discrimination, confidentiality and the rights of children and young people

Each setting will have a number of policies and procedures which directly relate to equality, diversity, discrimination, confidentiality, and the rights of children and young people.

Policies and procedures exist to ensure that everyone is aware of the agreed way of working within the organisation. Staff in particular will need to know the school's policies and procedures and refer to them if necessary when needed.

> **Inclusion** The process of identifying, understanding and breaking down barriers to participation and belonging.

Settings should have the policies (or policies with sections covering them) shown in Table 10.2.

Table 10.2 Links between legislation and the setting's policies and procedures

Policy	Link
Inclusion	This may be a standalone policy but might also link to the SEND or Equality and Diversity policy. It links both the Equality Act 2010 and the SEND Code of Practice 2015 to inclusion and the importance of promoting the involvement of all individuals.
Confidentiality	This policy outlines how the setting will keep to its obligations under UK GDPR, and protect and store information. It should also include details of how the setting will share information with other professionals where this is permitted and in a child's or young person's best interests, e.g. if they need to work with social services.

Check your understanding and progress at **www.hoddereducation.co.uk/myrevisionnotes**

Policy	Link
Accessibility/ access	The Equality Act 2010 requires that schools and other organisations should have an access policy or plan. This should complement the SEND and/or equal opportunities and inclusion policy, and set out the access arrangements for those with disabilities.

This policy should also state how the setting ensures equal access to the curriculum and wider context. |
| Partnership working | Safe partnership working may form part of the confidentiality policy.

This policy should explain that sharing information about children and young people should only be on a 'need to know' basis. It should also be linked to the SEND policy and Code of Practice, as professionals will need to know how to work together safely to improve outcomes. |
| Admissions | The admissions policy for schools and early years settings links to the SEND Code of Practice as well as the Equality Act; this is because it sets out the criteria for entry.

Under the SEND Code of Practice, children and young people who have an EHCP are able to specify their preferred school. |
| SEND | All schools and early years settings are required to have a policy for SEND under the 2015 SEND Code of Practice. This will outline the provision which the setting makes for children and young people with SEND. |
| Safeguarding | The setting's safeguarding policy will need to refer to several DfE guidance documents, including 'Keeping children safe in education part 1' and 'Working together to safeguard children'. It will set out the procedures which staff should follow in case of any safeguarding concerns. |

Now test yourself   TESTED ⬤

Which of the above policies might be linked to the following situations? Remember that there may be more than one policy in each case:

4 A child or young person who is in foster care where staff have concerns about her wellbeing.

5 A Year 6 girl who has asked if she can be in the boy's football team as there is no female equivalent in her school.

6 A family from a GRT (Gypsy Romani Traveller) background whose children have not received a place in a local school.

Making links

Element 3 sets out the legislation and statutory guidance around safeguarding. What is the key message of the Prevent Duty Guidance 2015?

This element and much of this legislation links to Element 11 on SEND. How and why does the Local Offer relate to the admissions policy?

Exam-style question

3 Which of these policies is *most* closely linked with UK GDPR? Choose one option.
   A accessibility policy
   B admissions policy
   C safeguarding policy
   D confidentiality policy
                                                              [1]

10.3 Why it is important to promote equality, diversity and inclusion

In addition to knowing about your setting's policies, it is important to be able to promote equality, diversity and inclusion in your work with children and young people. This is for a range of reasons:

+ **Complying with legal responsibilities (Equality Act 2010)**: everyone working in schools, colleges and early years settings is obliged by law to comply with their legal responsibilities under the Equality Act 2010 (see Section 10.1).
+ **Preventing discrimination**: both direct and indirect discrimination must be avoided, and challenged where it occurs.
+ **Ensuring equality of opportunity**: everyone is entitled to the same opportunities regarding access to activities and experiences.
+ **Meeting individual needs and ensuring accessibility for all**: adults should support children and young people in meeting their individual needs and allowing them to access the curriculum as well as the wider life of the setting.

119

+ **Appreciating and celebrating differences and valuing diversity**: acknowledging and valuing what makes people unique and distinct is important so that all children and young people develop a positive identity and learn to respect and value those of others.
+ **Recognising and valuing different family circumstances and cultures**: settings should recognise children's and young people's different family circumstances and backgrounds so that they can acknowledge and value them. It is essential not to make assumptions or judgements about the structure of their households or families. (See Element 5 for more on family structures.)
+ **Ensuring dignity and respect for all**: schools and early years settings should also promote positive images and messages around diversity, and use teaching and learning experiences which reflect the wider community.

Exam-style questions

4 Explain one reason why equality and diversity should be promoted in all schools and early years settings. [4]

5 Identify one action which schools and early years settings can take to promote equality, diversity and inclusion. [1]

Exam tip

Make sure you know the difference between the command words in the exam questions, such as 'Explain' and 'Identify'. These show you what kind of answer is expected – whether you have to simply give information, explain or describe it to show you understand, or even make a judgement on something (the question might also start with 'Analyse' or 'Discuss').

Figure 10.2 All adults are responsible for promoting equality of opportunity within schools and early years settings

10.4 The consequences of labelling children and young people

We sometimes hear of the term 'labelling' when talking about children and young people, particularly around SEND. Labels are also sometimes used by adults to identify or categorise their circumstances, for example, if they are looked after children, from a GRT (Gypsy Romani Traveller) background or eligible for the 'pupil premium'.

Although it can sometimes be helpful for adults to identify a child's or young person's needs and to consider strategies to support them, labels can also have negative connotations. Practitioners should always try to get to know each individual child before making assumptions about what they will or will not be able to do.

Pupil premium Money given by the government to schools to raise the attainment of disadvantaged pupils.

Figure 10.3 Why is it important to try to avoid labelling where possible?

Check your understanding and progress at **www.hoddereducation.co.uk/myrevisionnotes**

What are the effects of labelling?

Causes the individual to feel stigmatised

Feeling stigmatised means that the child or young person feels a sense of disapproval from others. This can cause them to lack self-esteem or have a low self-concept or self-image.

Changes how others view the individual

A label may affect how others see the child or young person, particularly if it has been applied in a negative way, or if they have a limited experience or understanding of the need or disability. Practitioners' views should be formed from knowledge and experience of the individual rather than preconceived ideas.

Establishes a set of limits associated with that label

Some people might see the label rather than the person first, and have limited expectations of what they will be able to do.

Places a burden of guilt or blame on the individual's parents/carers

Parents may already feel guilty or blame themselves for the circumstances which affect their child. Labelling may highlight this guilt and make it harder for them.

> **Making links**
>
> This section links to Element 4. Explain how a low self-concept might impact a child's or young person's behaviour and cognition.

Why it is important to have high and realistic expectations for children and young people

Having high and realistic expectations for children and young people will support them, raise their self-esteem and encourage them to achieve. If expectations are low, it will be harder for them to become motivated and as a result their achievements will be affected.

Positive expectations should include the following:

+ **Encourage independence**: making sure that practitioners encourage children and young people to do things for themselves which will improve their confidence.
+ **Increase motivation and confidence**: keeping a positive outlook, giving plenty of positive praise and using age-appropriate motivational tools will help to improve children's and young people's motivation and confidence in their own ability.
+ **Improve academic outcomes**: having high yet realistic expectations encourages children and young people to develop their own personal progress and improve their learning.
+ **Create a culture of achievement, regardless of ability**: children and young people are encouraged to put in effort and improve, whether or not they are naturally strong at something.

> **Now test yourself**   TESTED
>
> 7 Why might adults 'label' children and young people?
> 8 How might a label affect how others see the child or young person?
> 9 Identify two ways in which positive expectations can make a difference to children's and young people's achievements.

> **Exam-style question**
>
> 6 Explain three consequences of labelling children and young people.   [3]

10.5 The impact of a range of barriers to participation

Many different barriers may prevent children and young people from participating. These may range from physical barriers and a lack of resources to issues such as limited expectations of children and young people, mental health issues or socio-economic factors.

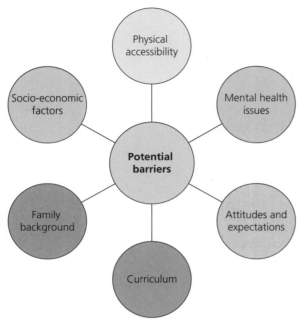

Figure 10.4 Potential barriers

> **AAC (augmentative and alternative communication)** This term is used to cover all types of communication methods that enhance or replace speech, such as sign language or technical devices.

> **Revision activity**
>
> See if you can recreate the spider diagram in Figure 10.4 from memory, and remember the impact of each barrier. Remember: this spider has only six legs!

Table 10.3 Impact of barriers to children's and young people's participation

Potential barrier	Impact of barrier
Physical accessibility	May occur if the learning environment does not have adequate resources in place for the age or needs of the children and young people. For example: + a child in a wheelchair who cannot access a school building + a pupil has communication issues but staff are not trained in using **AAC (augmentative and alternative communication)**. These pupils will be physically excluded from participating.
Mental health issues	May occur when a child or young person does not feel able to participate, lacks confidence, or is depressed or withdrawn. This may have long-term effects on their learning if it is not addressed.
Attitudes and expectations	The poor attitudes and low expectations of others may make a child or young person feel that they are unable to achieve. A positive attitude and high expectations are important for all children and young people, particularly those who may feel unmotivated or feel that they are unable to take part in an activity due to their gender, ethnicity, background or circumstances. A 'can do' attitude in those around them will support them in adapting this mindset.
Curriculum	The curriculum must be inclusive and meet the needs of all children and young people. This means: + taking all abilities, needs, backgrounds and cultures into account + recognising and celebrating diversity.
Family background	A child's or young person's family background may mean that they are not adequately supported by adults at home. An example would be if they come from an environment of abuse or neglect, or if they have to care for a parent. These factors will impact on how they feel about themselves and if they feel able to participate.
Socio-economic factors	If a child or young person comes from an environment which has limited resources or poor living conditions, this may affect their participation and involvement. They may be hungry, suffer from a lack of sleep due to housing issues or overcrowding, or be anxious about their situation. In addition, their family will find it more difficult to pay for extra-curricular activities.

Check your understanding and progress at **www.hoddereducation.co.uk/myrevisionnotes**

How to use strategies to overcome barriers to children's and young people's participation

Practitioners should be able to overcome barriers using different strategies to ensure the active participation of all children and young people. These may include the following:

✦ **Training to understand inclusion**: all members of the setting should be familiar with the inclusion policy and their part in implementing it. If assistants are working with an individual child or young person with SEND, they should have specific training to support this.

✦ **Partnership working, including supporting children's and young people's psychological wellbeing**: working closely with parents and other professionals will enable everyone to find out as much as they can about the child or young person and their needs. This will also help to ensure that there are suitable resources in place.

✦ **Adaptations to the physical environment**: if the child's or young person's needs are known about in advance, barriers in the physical environment can be overcome by making adaptations. For example, a hearing impaired child or young person in the class should have access to a hearing loop.

✦ **Providing an accessible curriculum/assessment**: the curriculum should be accessible to all children and young people, and they should have the resources they need to participate fully. This includes appropriate assessment so that they can understand their next steps for learning and make progress.

✦ **Reviewing equality, diversity and inclusion policies**: all policies should be reviewed on a regular basis to ensure that they are up to date and that all staff are aware of their contents.

✦ **Providing information to children and young people about financial support**: where children and young people need financial support, schools and early years settings should be able to give them additional information about how to access this.

✦ **Supporting children and young people through transitions**: support should be provided where children and young people are going through planned transitions such as starting school or going into a new class. This will help them to know in advance about the resources available to them.

Now test yourself
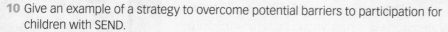

TESTED

10 Give an example of a strategy to overcome potential barriers to participation for children with SEND.

11 How might family background impact on the participation of a child or young person?

Making links

Transitions are also covered in Element 7. How many different kinds of planned and unplanned transitions can you list?

Exam-style question

7 Tom is eight years old, is severely visually impaired and has just started at a new school. He does not have a support assistant and his previous school have said that he manages his own needs well.

The school had several months' notice that Tom would be starting and have been able to plan to meet his needs. They have arranged for his teacher to meet the local sensory support team to discuss how they can support Tom. They have also made adaptations in the classroom and different areas of the school, and have additional resources to meet his needs as advised by the previous school. In addition, support has been put in place through the use of a 'buddy' as Tom gets to know his way around the classroom and school.

A Outline two barriers which Tom might have faced when starting at his new school. [2]

B Identify three ways in which the school has worked to overcome barriers to Tom's participation. [3]

123

11 Special educational needs and disability

All childcare and education practitioners will work with children and young people who have special educational needs and disabilities, as well as with their families. You should know about the different areas of need, how these may impact the child or young person, and where to find support in the setting and beyond.

11.1 The statutory duties and responsibilities of practitioners supporting children and young people with SEND and the link between the Children and Families Act 2014 and the SEND Code of Practice: 0 to 25 years 2015

The most important statutory document for practitioners when working with children and young people who have SEND (also known as SEN in many settings) is the SEND Code of Practice 2015. This document sets out the duties, policies and procedures that all organisations must follow when managing the care and education of children and young people with SEND.

In the case of children and young people who are home schooled, parents will need to be able to work in partnership with the local authority to ensure their needs are met.

The SEND Code of Practice was influenced by the Children and Families Act 2014, which introduced wide-ranging reforms to the areas of SEND, adoption, family courts and social care. These reforms highlighted a better need for co-operation between professionals when working with children and young people, and these were incorporated into the code. Some examples of this are:

+ the requirement for a Local Offer – a document which outlines what is available in the area for children and young people with SEND
+ joined-up services across education, health and care
+ the requirement for EHCPs; where the needs of children and young people cannot be met through normal provision, they may go through a process of assessment for an EHCP; this sets out the provision which must be put in place for the child or young person with SEND (see page 123)
+ SEND provision for young people in further education
+ a focus on preparing for adulthood and planning the transition to paid employment.

Figure 11.1 Each area of need is likely to have an impact on a child's or young person's development

Making links

This element links with Element 10, which is about equality and diversity. Under the SEND Code of Practice, what are the four broad areas of need for children and young people with SEND?

Check your understanding and progress at **www.hoddereducation.co.uk/myrevisionnotes**

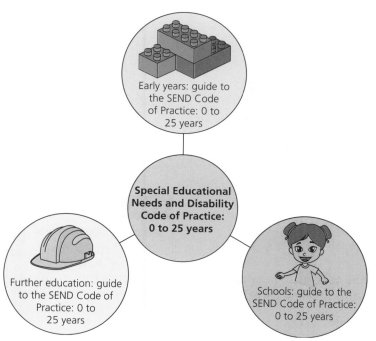

Figure 11.2 Special Educational Needs and Disability Code of Practice: 0 to 25 years

There are also three separate guidance documents, one for each age range, which break down the statutory duties and responsibilities of practitioners working with this age group. Each of these documents starts with the same headings and a short explanation.

Table 11.1 Explanation of headings in the guidance

Heading	Explanation
The context	The Children and Families Act 2014 and its statutory obligations, giving families more control over their child's welfare. (See also Element 3.)
Principles underlying the code	There are seven principles which must be observed by all professionals who work with children and young people who have SEND. They include ensuring the involvement of the children/young people and their parents/carers in decision-making about their needs and control over their support.
Working together	Under the Children and Families Act 2014, local authorities have a duty to ensure that all services work together to improve the quality of provision for children and young people with SEND.
The Local Offer	Local authorities must publish a Local Offer which outlines what is available for children and young people with SEND in the local area.

Explanation of the three guidance documents

REVISED ○

SEND: guide for early years settings

According to the EYFS Statutory Framework, all maintained nurseries and other early years providers who have funding from local authorities in England must work to the SEND Code of Practice 2015.

This guide highlights the main duties and responsibilities of early years providers, including the role of the SENDCo in early years provision.

SEND: guide for schools and alternative provision settings

Schools and alternative provision settings (where pupils are not in mainstream school) also have responsibilities under the Children and Families Act 2014. This guide focuses on a number of areas, including the identification of SEND in schools and improving outcomes for these children.

Further education: guide to the 0 to 25 SEND Code of Practice

This guide highlights the main duties and responsibilities of colleges. Its focus is on the following:

+ statutory duties of post-16 institutions
+ identifying and supporting young people in college
+ preparing for adulthood
+ young people's right to make their own decisions concerning their future
+ planning the transition into post-16 education, training and careers advice
+ pathways to employment.

> **Exam tip**
>
> You do not need to know all of the seven principles underlying the Code of Practice but it will be useful to know at least one or two. There are four in Table 11.1.

> **Now test yourself**   TESTED ◯
>
> 1 Identify which guidance document sets out the duties, policies and procedures for *all* organisations in relation to SEND.
> 2 Which law influenced this guidance document?
> 3 Identify three of the main duties and responsibilities of colleges.

The purpose of a range of organisational policies and procedures that support children and young people with SEND

REVISED ◯

Organisational policies are designed to set out an agreed way of working for all. The policies in Table 11.2 are in place to support children and young people in the setting with SEND.

Table 11.2 Policies and procedures that support children and young people with SEND

Policy	Purpose
SEND	This policy sets out how the school, college or early years setting will support children and young people with SEND. + Aims and objectives should be clear, and outline the procedures to follow when identifying, assessing and providing support for SEND. + It should also provide guidance for parents.
Equality	This should set out: + the organisation's commitment to equality and anti-discriminatory practice + how it will meet the requirements of the Equality Act 2010.
Accessibility	A legal requirement of the Equality Act 2010 is that organisations should have an accessibility or access policy. This will demonstrate: + how the setting will meet the access requirements of those with disabilities + how it makes provision for equal access to the curriculum and other activities which the school or early years setting provides, such as clubs.
Alternative provision	This policy sets out what a mainstream school will do in cases where a child or young person is unable to attend due to emotional, behaviour or health reasons. This may be linked to SEND where pupils have specific needs. Note: it does not apply to early years settings.

Policy	Purpose
Anti-bullying	This may be part of the behaviour policy. It should set out: + what the setting has in place to prevent all types of bullying among children and young people + the roles of staff and parents if bullying occurs.
Behaviour	All schools and early years settings will have a policy for behaviour (for more on this, see Element 4). In the context of SEND, changes in behaviour can be an indicator that the child's or young person's needs are not being met in some way. Behaviour policies should outline the kinds of adaptations which should be made for pupils with SEND so that they have achievable targets for behaviour.
Medical needs	This area may have its own policy or may be part of the first aid or health and safety policy. It will set out the setting's requirements for children and young people with healthcare and medical needs and conditions, for example, administering medicines.
Teaching and learning	This policy sets out how the school or early years setting provides activities and opportunities for each child or young person. These should meet their individual needs through a differentiated curriculum.
Complaints	This policy exists so that parents are able to raise concerns if needed. It should set out a clear procedure for both sides to follow in case of any complaint.

Now test yourself   TESTED ⬤

4 Describe what organisational policies are designed to do.
5 Name four policies which organisations may have in place to set out provision for children and young people with SEND.
6 Explain the purpose of the policies you have chosen and how they support children and young people with SEND.

Revision activity

Copy the grid of Table 11.2 and the column of policy names. See if you can write out the right-hand column of the table to outline the purpose of each policy.

The available support in childcare, schools and colleges for children and young people with SEND

REVISED ⬤

In addition to what is set out in the SEND Code of Practice, children and young people who have SEND will also be entitled to at least the support shown in Table 11.3, at different stages.

Table 11.3 Available support for children and young people with SEND

Age	Available support
0 to 5 years	+ A written progress check at two to three years. + A child's health visitor carrying out a health check for children aged two to three. + A written assessment in the summer term of a child's first year of primary school (known as the EYFS Profile). + **Reasonable adjustments** for children with disabilities (this is true for all age groups).
5 to 15 years	+ A special learning programme (to focus on a pupil's weaknesses). + Extra help from a teacher, teaching assistant or mental health lead. + Opportunities to work in smaller groups or other areas of the school if needed. + Observation in class or at break. + Help taking part in class activities. + Extra encouragement in their learning, for example, to ask questions or to try something they find difficult. + Help communicating with other children or young people (for example, with AAC – see Section 11.11). + Support with physical or personal care difficulties, for example, eating, getting around school safely or using the toilet.

127

Early Help Assessment (EHA)

+ EHAs provide a means of putting in place early support, in partnership with relevant professionals, as soon as issues arise.
+ EHAs can be used from Early Years through school years.

EHCPs

+ EHCPs are intended to support children and young people with complex needs that fall outside the SEND provision provided by childcare, schools or colleges.
+ A parent/carer can request an EHCP if they think it is appropriate for their child.
+ A young person can request an assessment themselves if they are aged 16 to 25.

> **Reasonable adjustment**
> A change which is made to reduce the disadvantage which a person has due to their disability.

Exam-style questions

1 Identify two different types of support available to pupils with SEND between 5 and 15 years old. [2]
2 Explain the purpose of an EHCP and who can request one. [4]
3 What is the name of the written assessment which takes place at the end of the EYFS? [1]
4 Why are EHAs important? [1]

11.2 How professionals and organisations support children and young people with SEND

Teachers

REVISED ○

Teachers and early years practitioners support the individual needs of all children and young people, but will need to provide additional support to enable those with SEND to access the curriculum.

Figure 11.3 How can adults help children and young people with an identified SEN to access the curriculum?

For those with an identified SEN

Special educational provision will need to be made for these children or young people in the setting. They will have specific targets and support in place, co-ordinated by the teacher and SENDCo. The child's or young person's parents will be involved, along with any other professionals who have given support.

For those who do not have an identified SEN

If a child or young person does not have an identified SEN but parents and practitioners have a cause for concern:

+ First, teachers should discuss this with parents or carers, and document the discussion.
+ They should also raise the awareness of the SENDCo.
+ In addition, teachers and early years practitioners will need to differentiate the child's or young person's work and educational experiences appropriately.

Teachers should then:

+ review the progress of the child or young person
+ speak regularly to parents and the SENDCo
+ involve them in setting up any assessments with other professionals.

> **Differentiate** To tailor instructions and set work according to the needs/level of children and young people.

Educational psychologists

REVISED

These are professionals who are trained in psychology and child development. They can:

+ assess the educational needs of children and young people
+ provide support and advice to parents, teachers and early years professionals.

Medical practitioners

REVISED

Medical practitioners may be involved in supporting children and young people if they have health or medical needs; for example, if they have a medical condition such as muscular dystrophy and have an EHCP.

Medical practitioners and the local paediatric team will be involved in advising the school or early years setting in how best to meet the child's needs. They are also likely to be involved in reviews which will take place annually.

The role of a multi-agency team in providing integrated support for children and young people with SEND

REVISED

A multi-agency team may comprise a range of health professionals, youth workers, social workers and those who work in mental health, as well as teachers or early years practitioners.

Their role is to ensure that children and young people who have SEND receive co-ordinated support more quickly. They will work alongside the child or young person and their family, so that their thoughts and opinions will be included in any decision-making.

Now test yourself TESTED

7 Name one type of professional who may support a child or young person with SEND.

8 How should an early years worker or teacher support a child or young person where they have concerns but the child or young person does not have an identified SEN?

9 What might an educational psychologist do to support a child or young person?

11.3 The principles of integration, equity and inclusion, and the differences between them

You will need to understand clearly how these principles differ.

+ The principle of integration separates the needs of SEND pupils in a way that is distinct from the needs of others.
+ The principle of equity relates to a fair curriculum as well as strong partnerships with parents and the promotion of social cohesion.
+ The principle of inclusion encompasses the needs of all children and young people, including those who have SEND.

Table 11.4 How the principles of integration and inclusion differ

Principle of integration	Principle of inclusion	Principle of equity
Children and young people with SEND require separate support and extra resources to access the curriculum.	A curriculum should offer all students equal rights, access and choices. This means making reasonable adjustments in advance to enable all children and young people to participate wherever possible.	The curriculum is fair, and children's/young people's holistic development needs are well planned for. This means that all areas of the curriculum should be considered.
The success of children and young people depends on their ability to adapt to the learning environment.	The learning environment should be adapted to support the success of each child and young person in the setting.	Social cohesion is promoted and children/young people learn to connect with one another. This means that in the learning environment all children and young people have equal opportunities.
Extra adaptations and support within the learning environment should only benefit those with SEND.	Extra adaptations and support within the learning environment can benefit everyone.	

In addition, the principles of equity promote a sense of fairness in the following ways:

+ The educator must understand their own culture, personal values and biases. This means that they should think about why their thoughts and opinions might have been fixed in a certain way.
+ Partnerships with parents should be strong, with shared aspirations for children and young people. This means that educators and parents should communicate to share thoughts and ideas as much as possible.

Figure 11.4 What kinds of adjustments might be made to support pupils with SEND?

Check your understanding and progress at **www.hoddereducation.co.uk/myrevisionnotes**

Now test yourself TESTED ⚪

10 What is meant by the term 'reasonable adjustment'?

11 Which of the principles of equity relates to partnerships with parents and what does it mean?

Exam-style question

5 Max is working in a large secondary school and supports pupils in the maths department. In one of his groups is a Year 7 pupil, Bhumika, who has an EHCP due to a chronic health condition. Max knows that her health condition is cystic fibrosis, and that she is a wheelchair user and is able to move around the school in her chair. However, Max has just heard that Bhumika will not be attending the Year 7 trip because the school has not found an adult to accompany her.

A Discuss why this might be a cause for concern and why Bhumika should be able to go on the trip. [6]

B Explain how the school might work with Bhumika's parents to find a solution? [4]

11.4 Appropriate terminology to use when discussing the needs of children and young people with SEND

It is important to use appropriate terminology when describing and discussing the needs of children and young people with SEND. Negative terminology can be both hurtful and damaging, and highlight the disability or need rather than the individual. It is part of the adult's role to enable the child or young person, rather than contribute to singling them out.

Table 11.5 gives some common examples of inappropriate terms or phrasing and the preferred alternative(s).

Table 11.5 Inappropriate and preferred terms or phrasings

Inappropriate term or phrasing	Preferred term or phrasing
Disabled person (emphasis on individual)	Person with a disability
Suffers from (implies discomfort or despair)	Has or lives with
Confined to a wheelchair (implies that the individual is a victim)	Wheelchair user/uses a wheelchair
Colloquial language to describe a symptom of a disability or medical condition (e.g. fits or spells)	The relevant medical terms (e.g. seizure)

Why practitioners must use appropriate terminology when discussing the needs of children and young people with SEND

REVISED ⚪

Practitioners must use appropriate terminology when discussing the needs of children and young people with SEND for several reasons:

+ **Complying with organisational policies**: the SEND and equality policies are likely to highlight the use of appropriate terminology as a requirement.
+ **Avoiding stereotyping or labelling**: it is important that practitioners do not make assumptions about what children and young people can or cannot do. Stereotyping and labelling can be demoralising and have a negative impact on the achievements of children and young people, particularly those who have SEND. (See also Section 10.4, page 116.)

131

+ **Valuing and respecting individuals**: using appropriate language and terminology is an important part of appreciating all individuals for themselves and protecting their rights.
+ **Maintaining professionalism**: practitioners should use the correct terms as this is part of appropriate behaviour when working with children and young people with SEND and their families.

Now test yourself   TESTED ⬤

12 Give two reasons why you should use appropriate terminology when discussing the needs of children and young people with SEND.

Exam-style question

6 Which one of these is not an appropriate term when discussing the needs of a child or young person with SEND?
   A wheelchair user
   B suffers from
   C person with a disability
   D seizure   [1]

11.5 The difference between the medical and social models of disability

In the past, children and young people with disabilities have been educated separately from their peers. This was mainly because a disability was often seen as a problem belonging to the individual.

The social model of disability was developed in the 1980s. It advocates thinking of disability as being created by society, and to think about how society can be organised so that people with disabilities can participate rather than be excluded by default. This model changed access and participation for people with disabilities and continues to challenge society to remove barriers to participation.

The relationship between the medical and social models of disability is similar to that of the principles of integration and inclusion, in that the child or young person with SEND should not be the one who needs to make changes.

Table 11.6 Relationship between the medical and social models of disability

Medical model	Social model
Child is faulty	Child is valued
Diagnosis	Strengths and needs defined by self and others
Labelling	Identifies barriers and develops solutions
Impairment becomes focus of attention	Outcome-based programme designed
Assessment, monitoring, programmes of therapy imposed	Resources are made available to ordinary services
Segregation and alternative services	Training for parents and professionals
Ordinary needs put on hold	Relationships nurtured
Re-entry if 'normal' enough, or permanent exclusion	Diversity welcomed, child is included
Society remains unchanged	Society evolves

Source: Mason, M and Rieser, R (1994) *Altogether Better (From 'Special Needs' to Equality in Education)*. Charity Projects/Comic Relief, p.188

Exam-style question

7 Explain the difference between the medical and social models of disability.   [4]

Check your understanding and progress at **www.hoddereducation.co.uk/myrevisionnotes**

11.6 How a primary disability may affect development

A primary disability is likely to affect a child's or young person's development in many areas. This is because they are still growing and developing, and a disability in one area will impact on others.

Remember that a disability:
+ may not always be visible to other people
+ may be short-term, for example, in the case of an illness or accident.

Table 11.7 shows how a primary disability may affect social and emotional development and physical development.

> **Primary disability** The main physical or mental impairment that has a negative effect on a person's ability to carry out normal activities. The individual may have other impairments resulting from or apart from this.

Table 11.7 Impact of the primary disability on development

Area of development	Impact of the primary disability on development
	Impact on social and emotional development
Impulse control	A child's or young person's primary disability might affect their ability to control their emotions and impulses.
Language development	A child or young person might become frustrated by their needs and have problems in communicating them.
Mood and emotion	A disability might be overwhelming for the child or young person. They might need support in managing emotions such as frustration or anger.
	Impact on physical development
Attention and concentration/memory	+ If a disability causes physical pain or discomfort, this may also affect a child's or young person's concentration. + They may also be taking medication which can lead to tiredness and affect their memory. + A cognitive difficulty can affect concentration and memory, as it might take longer for a child or young person to learn new skills and remember them.
Sensory processing	This can be a feature of autistic spectrum conditions. Children or young people might have difficulties in filtering out sensory information such as noises in the environment, and can become 'overloaded' by too much stimulation.
Motor control	If the primary disability is in the area of physical development, this might affect how the person controls their movements or speech. Motor control might also be affected if there is a cognitive difficulty which impacts processing skills.

Now test yourself   TESTED ◯

13 What is meant by the term 'primary disability'?
14 Name three ways in which a primary disability might affect physical development.

> **Sensory processing** The way in which an individual receives and processes information through the senses.

Exam-style question

8 Lucy is in Year 3 and has broken her leg in an accident. She had been looking forward to being a bridesmaid at her aunt's wedding, and was about to take a dance exam when the accident happened.

  A Describe how different areas of Lucy's development may be affected by the accident. [4]

  B Discuss how her school could support her in these areas. [6]

11.7 The range of cognitive skills necessary for effective educational development, and how single or multiple disabilities might affect these

Cognitive skills are necessary for effective educational development, as they enable a person to:

+ focus their attention
+ remember information and process it
+ apply their knowledge in different situations.

A person who has neurological or neurodevelopmental disabilities is likely to find the development of these skills challenging to a greater or lesser extent.

> **Neurological** Relating to or affecting the brain and nervous system.
>
> **Neurodevelopmental** Relating to the development of the central nervous system, for example, in the case of autistic spectrum conditions.

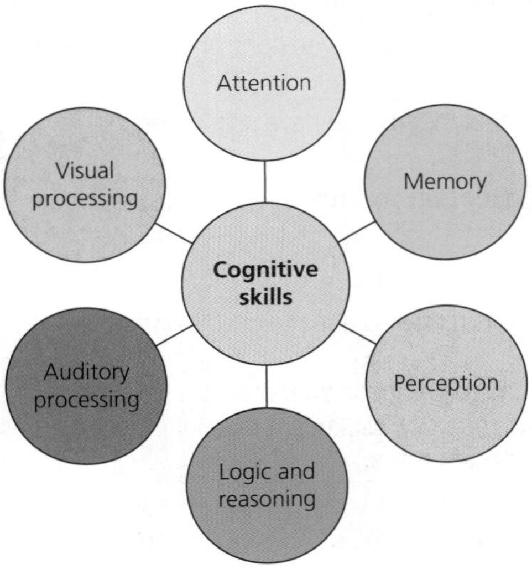

Figure 11.5 Cognitive skills

Cognitive skills include the following:

+ **Attention**: the child or young person might not be able to sustain their attention for as long as their peers.
+ **Memory (short- and long-term)**: it might be harder for the child or young person to remember what they have already learnt about a subject or topic. They might need support to do this.
+ **Perception**: this is a more abstract concept, which involves being able to work something out using available information. Those with some disabilities might find this harder to do.
+ **Logic and reasoning**: this involves being able to make connections, for example, when problem-solving and thinking about why things happen.
+ **Auditory and visual processing**: this involves interpreting information through sounds and images. The child or young person will not have an auditory or visual impairment, but will find it difficult to make sense of the information they receive.

> **Typical mistakes**
>
> Remember that children and young people who have auditory and visual processing difficulties do not have an auditory or visual impairment: they just have difficulties in making sense of the information they receive.
>
> Individuals with auditory difficulties might have problems processing speech and responding appropriately.
>
> Those with visual processing difficulties might have problems with spatial processing, judging distances, or the way in which they see shapes and symbols.

> **Exam-style question**
>
> 9 Which one of these is not a cognitive skill necessary for effective educational development?
>   A motor control
>   B logic and reasoning
>   C auditory processing
>   D perception   [1]

Check your understanding and progress at **www.hoddereducation.co.uk/myrevisionnotes**

11.8 How cognitive difficulties might have an impact on language, communication and educational development

Cognitive difficulties might also have an impact on language, communication and educational development. This is because a child or young person will need to have:

✚ a good working memory in order to remember vocabulary and language
✚ the processing skills needed to understand and use language, and organise their thoughts.

Table 11.8 Impact of cognitive difficulties

Area of skill	Area and impact of difficulty
Reading/writing/comprehension	Children and young people who have cognitive difficulties might take longer to process information, and so language skills might take longer to develop. They are also likely to find reading and writing more challenging, and will find comprehension questions harder if they are asked to look beyond the text.
Mathematical skills/concepts	Mathematical skills and concepts will often require logical and abstract thought, and applying existing knowledge in different ways. Children and young people who have cognitive difficulties might need support in talking through how to do this.
Vocabulary and communication	It might be harder for children and young people with cognitive difficulties to remember specific vocabulary relating to a subject or topic. They might also find it harder to articulate their thoughts and communicate them to others.
Attention span	It will be more difficult for children and young people with cognitive difficulties to concentrate and hold their attention on learning activities. This will make it harder for them to sustain their thinking when carrying out tasks.
Co-ordination	Children and young people with cognitive difficulties may also have problems with co-ordinating their motor skills. ✚ Fine motor skills might include handwriting, tying laces or carrying out more detailed work. ✚ Gross motor skills include running and jumping, so this will affect larger movements.
Logical reasoning	This relates to a person's ability to make connections and think about what to do next in their learning. Those with cognitive difficulties are likely to find this more difficult.
Memory/building on prior knowledge	When we are learning, we build on prior knowledge before moving on to the next thing. Those who have cognitive difficulties might find it harder to do this.

Now test yourself   TESTED ⬤

15 Why might cognitive difficulties impact on language and communication?
16 How might cognitive difficulties impact on a person's ability to develop mathematical skills?

Making links

Element 7 also looks at language and cognitive development. Name two theorists who produced work on children's language development.

11.9 How a chronic condition may affect emotions, education, behaviour and quality of life

A chronic health condition is one which is long-standing, and may often be lifelong. It is therefore likely to affect a person in various ways.

Although some chronic conditions can be controlled with medication, this may also cause side effects. Practitioners should be aware of the individual's needs and what their condition involves.

Muscular dystrophy

REVISED

This is a progressive condition which can mean that a person's life expectancy is significantly reduced.

As the condition worsens, the individual will find it harder to control their physical movements. They may also have frustrations and anxieties about the future, which will affect their emotions and make it harder to concentrate on everyday tasks.

Epilepsy

REVISED

This is a neurological condition which causes seizures. These may be very regular or quite rare, and can in many cases be controlled by medication.

The child or young person will be affected in different ways, depending on the severity of the condition; for example, anxiety about having a seizure, or being wary about taking part in some activities.

Figure 11.6 How might a chronic condition affect a child or young person in their day-to-day life?

Severe allergies

REVISED

These may be triggered in different ways, for example, in the environment, such as hay fever, or through specific foods, such as nuts.

Severe allergies can be very dangerous and in some cases life-threatening if not treated immediately. Having a severe allergy might cause a child or young person to have anxiety about what will happen if they have an episode.

Cystic fibrosis

REVISED

This is a genetic condition which affects how salt and water move in and out of cells in the body, and affects the lungs and digestive system.

The individual might look healthy, but is likely to need a range of treatments.

A child or young person who has cystic fibrosis might need emotional as well as physical support. They might become tired easily and find it hard to focus.

Depression

REVISED

Depression can affect emotions and behaviour, as well as academic work. It can cause eating disorders, self-harm, drug or alcohol abuse, and withdrawal from others.

Check your understanding and progress at **www.hoddereducation.co.uk/myrevisionnotes**

Fragile X syndrome

REVISED

Fragile X is an inherited condition that causes learning disabilities.

A child or young person with Fragile X might have a short attention span and be impulsive, and have social and emotional or communication problems. They might also share some features of autistic spectrum conditions, such as social anxiety and difficulties relating to others.

Sickle cell disease

REVISED

This is the name given to a group of inherited disorders that affect the shape of red blood cells. This causes painful episodes called sickle cell crises (singular: crisis), as well as tiredness, shortness of breath and anaemia, and emotional effects.

It is most common among people who are from an African or Caribbean background, and can also cause growth delay and a greater risk of serious infections. Sickle cell disease can cause a child or young person to have absences from the setting.

> **Anaemia** A health condition in which there are not enough red blood cells in the body, meaning the body might not receive enough oxygen.

Diabetes

REVISED

A chronic condition in which sugar levels build up in the blood and become too high because the body is unable to produce insulin or becomes resistant to it. There are two types of diabetes:

+ **Type 1 diabetes** often runs in families and is a lifelong condition. It can be present from birth or emerge later in life. In Type 1 diabetes, the immune system destroys the insulin-producing cells in the body.

  Treatment: the condition is managed by injecting insulin, with food or drink, to keep glucose at a safe level.

+ **Type 2 diabetes** can develop at any time and can be linked to poor diet and lack of exercise. In Type 2 diabetes, the body does not produce enough insulin, or the cells in the body become resistant to it. Type 2 diabetes is far more common than Type 1 among adults with diabetes.

  Treatment: the condition can sometimes be managed through diet and exercise alone, although it may also be controlled by medication.

In each case, diabetes will need to be closely managed and monitored as it can also cause other health conditions.

Now test yourself

TESTED

17 Identify at least one chronic health condition and state how it may affect a child or young person.

18 How might muscular dystrophy impact on a child's or young person's emotions and quality of life?

11.10 How adults can remove barriers in order to empower and value children and young people

When supporting children and young people with SEND, it is particularly important for adults in schools and early years settings to promote their independence and remove any barriers to their learning.

As far as possible and depending on their needs, children and young people should not develop an over-reliance on others to do things for them if they are able to do these things for themselves.

> **Making links**
>
> Element 10 also discusses the impacts of barriers to learning. What are some of the potential barriers caused by mental health issues?

137

Table 11.9 Strategies for removing barriers

What adults can do to remove barriers	How they can do this
Create an accessible and secure environment	Provide access to all areas of the learning environment, and make adaptations where necessary.
	Children and young people should have access to any specific materials or resources they may need, and staff should also be trained in their use.
	All health, safety and security issues should have been met for all pupils.
Promote value and respect	The equality policy should promote the principles of value and respect in the setting, and this should apply to everyone.
	Adults should also be role models in the way in which they treat others.
Involve the individual in planning	Children and young people should be involved from an early age in making self-assessments of their learning and thinking about what they need to do next.
	For those with SEND, involvement in meetings and talking to adults about their learning targets and healthcare needs will support the development of their independence.
Provide context and relevance to learning	This involves the child or young person being able to make connections between their learning and its relevance to their lives.
	Those with SEND might find this harder than others, so it is important for adults to support them in making these connections.
Use **enabling language**	The use of enabling language is very important for children and young people who have SEND. They might feel restricted and unable to carry out tasks and activities, or have low self-esteem.
Work with the family and others	All educators must work with parents and other professionals when supporting children and young people with SEND. This is because it is the best way to gain knowledge and understanding of the needs of the child.
Implement policies and procedures	All adults must ensure that they know and comply with the relevant policies and procedures when working with children and young people who have SEND. (See Section 11.1 for a list of these.)

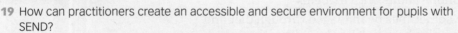

Now test yourself TESTED ◯

19 How can practitioners create an accessible and secure environment for pupils with SEND?

20 How can adults promote the principles of values and respect for pupils with SEND in the setting?

> **Enabling language** Using language which makes the individual feel that they are able to do something.

Exam-style questions

10 It is important to know about and implement policies and procedures which are relevant to SEND when working with children and young people. Identify three relevant policies and procedures. [3]

11 Rachel is working in Year 4 with Anton, who has moderate cognition and learning needs. They are looking at a problem-solving exercise in maths, but Anton lacks confidence in his own ability and says he doesn't know what to do.

A Describe how Rachel can encourage Anton through the use of enabling language. [4]

B Explain why it is important that she does this rather telling him what to do. [4]

11.11 When and how speech can be supplemented or replaced by AAC

Communication is a key part of teaching and learning as it enables us to share information. It is also the way in which we express ourselves and develop relationships with others.

For children and young people who have communication needs, it is important for practitioners to enable them to communicate and express themselves as much as possible. There are three different ways to achieve this.

Check your understanding and progress at **www.hoddereducation.co.uk/myrevisionnotes**

No-tech communication

This involves the use of gestures, body language, signing, pointing and facial expressions to support communication. Objects of reference and vocalisations might also be used to help to convey meaning.

Low-tech communication systems

Low-tech usually means AAC, which does not involve any power or battery in order to function. This may mean that pen and paper, picture exchange communication systems (PECS) using symbols or photographs are used. Low-tech systems give children and young people a starting point when receiving information so that it is easier to process and understand.

> **AAC (augmentative and alternative communication)** This term is used to cover all types of communication methods that enhance or replace speech, such as sign language or technical devices.

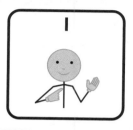

 want

 need

 more

 snack

 drink

Figure 11.7 The PECS method of communication uses a series of simple pictures

High-tech communication systems

These forms of communication are for individuals who need support in producing speech sounds. Systems could include mobile devices, laptops, tablets, speech synthesis, or eye-tracking devices.

A system might be recommended by a speech therapist or AAC specialist, and will be used to address the needs and requirements of the individual, for example, using their head or eyes.

In some cases, high-tech communication systems might also involve the use of voice output communication aids (VOCAs), which produce the sound of a voice.

Now test yourself
TESTED

21 Give an example of a low-tech communication system.
22 When would a high-tech communication system be used?
23 What is no-tech communication?

Revision activity

Under each heading, No-tech, Low-tech and High-tech communication, list as many communication systems as you can.

Exam-style question

12 Rhodri is six years old, has a diagnosis of an autistic spectrum condition and is non-verbal (does not speak). He has a support assistant who works with him in class, and he uses PECS to communicate what he wants to say. His parents, who work closely with the school, have said that they would like him to develop other communication systems to support him, and the SENDCo has set up a meeting to talk about the options.

Discuss what communication systems might be available to Rhodri, and evaluate their use in his situation.

[6]

12 English as an additional language

Many children come into education settings with a home language other than English (with EAL). Understanding how children learn English alongside a home language and also how best to support them is the focus for this unit.

EAL English as an additional language.

12.1 The characteristics of the five stages of acquiring an additional language

You need to know the five stages in which children and young people become fluent in another language.

Table 12.1 Five stages of acquiring an additional language

Stage	Features
Silent/receptive stage	+ Continued use of home language until realisation that others do not understand them. + Child or young person starts to understand random words or phrases but does not say anything in new language.
Early production	+ Use of single words or 'set' simple phrases (e.g. good morning) gained as a result of frequent exposure.
Speech emergence	+ Starting to attempt words or simple phrases spontaneously, e.g. 'It's big!'
Intermediate **fluency**	+ Increased use of simple English. + Sentences are short and vocabulary limited.
Continued language development/advanced fluency	+ Increased fluency and confidence in using new language. + Vocabulary continues to expand. + Increased ability to think in new language.

Early production Being able to say or repeat some words.

Fluency Being able to understand and use a language quickly and easily.

It is important to be able to recognise these stages for the following reasons:
+ Correct identification means that practitioners can use appropriate strategies to support the child or young person.
+ Practitioners can use them to track the progress of a child or young person.
+ Practitioners can then seek advice if a child or young person is not showing progress.

Revision activity

Make five flashcards.
+ On one side, write the stage of acquiring another language.
+ On the reverse, write the corresponding bullet points from Table 12.1.
+ Shuffle the cards then select one.
+ Can you either identify the stage from the bullet points, or remember the bullet points linked to the stage?

Now test yourself TESTED

1 Explain why it is important for a practitioner to be able to recognise a child's or young person's stage of EAL.
2 Identify the features of the silent/receptive stage.
3 Give an example of speech during the early production stage of acquiring an additional language.

Exam-style question

1 Abass is 14 years old. His family are refugees from Iraq. This is his fourth week in school. He has started to say a few words and phrases, including 'Bye' and 'Yes, that's okay'.
   A Identify his current stage of acquiring English. [1]
   B Explain what the next steps in learning English are likely to be for Abass. [4]

Check your understanding and progress at **www.hoddereducation.co.uk/myrevisionnotes**

12.2 How a range of factors might affect language acquisition

Exam tip

Learning the different factors is essential, as questions linked to a case study might be part of the exam.

The speed at which an individual gains a new language is determined by a number of factors. Eight different factors are given in the specification. To make it easier to learn, you can split them into three categories:

1 personal factors
2 family factors
3 education factors.

Bilingualism The ability to use more than one language.

Table 12.2 Factors that might affect language acquisition

Factor	How this affects language acquisition
Personal factors affecting language acquisition	
Age and development stage	Older children and young people are faster to pick up a new language. This is because their cognitive skills are more advanced, allowing them to remember new words and also analyse how languages are working.
	Their home language is also established, and this acts as a foundation for acquiring further languages.
Personality	Sociable and curious children and young people are more motivated to communicate and are less fearful about making mistakes. This allows them to make faster progress.
Cognition	Learning a new language requires memory and information processing skills. Children and young people who are quick to learn have an advantage.
SEND	Children and young people who have a learning difficulty or disability that affects communication – e.g. hearing difficulty – might need a longer time to learn a new language.
Family factors affecting language acquisition	
Bilingualism	Children and young people who have already mastered more than one language at home might be quicker to learn a new language.
Cultural background	Whether the child's or young person's family attitude towards education and learning English is positive is an important factor in how inclined they are to learn.
Education factors affecting language acquisition	
Learning environment	The resources, the attitudes of peers and teachers and the use of English in the education setting can help a child or young person learn more quickly.
Available support	The more support a child or young person has, the quicker they can learn.

Figure 12.1 How can personal and home factors affect the acquisition of another language?

Revision activity

+ Divide a piece of paper into three. Write down the following headings – one in each section: family, personal and education.
+ Write at least one factor under each of the headings. (Remember: there are eight factors altogether in the specification.) Check your answers against Table 12.2.

141

Now test yourself   TESTED ◯

4 Explain how personality might affect a child's or young person's acquisition of another language.

5 Identify two factors that might positively affect a young person's acquisition of English.

6 Explain the impact of existing bilingualism on a child's or young person's acquisition of language.

Exam tip

Make sure that your answer shows that no two children or young people will have exactly the same experience of EAL.

Exam-style question

2 Naseer is 12 years old. He is very sociable and likes team games such as basketball. His family are keen for him to learn English, and there have always been a lot of books in his home.

Consider the factors that might impact positively on Naseer's acquisition of English. [6]

Typical mistake

Don't answer a question as if EAL is a form of SEND. While some children and young people may also have SEND, EAL and SEND are not connected.

12.3 How home language affects education and development

This outcome is about the impact of a home language on education and development. The impact can be positive as well as negative.

Table 12.3 How home language affects education and development

	Positive impact of a home language on education and development	Negative impact of a home language on education and development
Their understanding of language overall	Children and young people who have a strong home language find it easier to learn a new language, and so make progress in education.	Children and young people who have not mastered the home language find it hard to make good progress to learn a new language, and this will affect their progress overall.
Family connections and support network	Where children and young people are fluent in their home language, they can interact with their parents and wider family members more fully and so develop a strong sense of identity.	Where children and young people are not yet fluent in the home language, this can cause tensions within the family. Children and young people might not be able to participate in family celebrations and rituals because they cannot interact easily with family members who do not speak English.
Self-concept	They may develop a positive self-concept because they are able to speak more than one language.	They may develop a negative self-concept if they cannot use the home language fluently and this is a source of shame or disappointment for their family. They may develop a negative self-concept if their peer group and the wider community do not view their home language as being valuable.
Their social interactions and relationships	Children and young people might find it easier to interact with others who also have a home language that is not English, as they have something in common.	Some children and young people might face discrimination and bullying because they are seen as different by their peers.
How they learn a curriculum	Cognitive advantages to being bilingual might result in some children and young people finding it easier to process information and so make good progress.	If they have vocabulary gaps or are not yet fluent in English, they might not be able to understand everything and fully participate. This will affect their ability to make progress.
Their acquisition of additional languages	Children and young people who are bilingual will find it easier to learn English and other languages that may form part of the curriculum.	Children and young people might not see the relevance of learning another language, such as French or Spanish, as part of the curriculum as they might not have mastered English or they might prefer to gain a qualification that recognises their home language.

Check your understanding and progress at **www.hoddereducation.co.uk/myrevisionnotes**

Making links

+ Read Element 4, Section 4.4. Give one example of how negative self-concept may affect a child's cognition.
+ Read Element 7, Section 7.5. Explain how having a home language may make a young person part of an 'out-group'.

Revision activity

Write a list of the positive ways in which having a home language might impact a child's or young person's education and development.

Now test yourself TESTED ⬤

7 What might be the impact of a different home language on the development of a positive self-concept?

8 Give an example of how a child's or young person's home language might affect their family connections and/or support network.

9 How might having a different home language to the language of the setting affect a child's or young person's acquisition of another language?

Exam tip

Remember that some factors combine, so outcomes can be different for each child or young person. For example, an isolated speaker of another language might be quicker to pick up English as they cannot speak to anyone else in their own language, while being with others who speak the home language may be helpful emotionally.

Exam-style question

3 Evaluate the potential impact on a child's or young person's self-concept and social interactions when their peer group does not value their home language. [6]

12.4 The communication, social and emotional needs of children/young people being taught EAL

Children's and young people's progress in education settings can be affected by their communication and social and emotional needs.

Communication needs

REVISED ⬤

Four main communication needs are given in the specification, but there may be others.

Table 12.4 Communication needs

Communication need	Effect
Children/young people might be more proficient in spoken than written English	+ They might need longer to write things down. + Teachers might underestimate the child's or young person's knowledge and understanding. + They might lose interest in lessons where there are many written tasks.
Children/young people might have difficulty understanding the curriculum	+ They might miss out on some aspects of a lesson. + They might misunderstand meanings of words or concepts. + They might lose interest in lessons. + Teachers might assume that a child or young person has SEND.
Children/young people might have difficulty accessing resources in English	+ Lack of books or resources in English at home might result in homework not being completed. + Teachers might think that the child or young person is not motivated.
Children/young people might have difficulty responding to questions in English	+ They might understand but need longer to formulate answers. + They might not participate in lessons where quick responses are needed. + They might start to withdraw. + Teachers might think that a child or young person is not interested or has not understood.

REVISED ●

Revision activity

See if you can complete Table 12.4 from memory. Then go back and see whether you have missed anything.

Communication need	Effect
Children/young people might be more proficient in spoken than written English	
	+ They might miss out on some aspects of a lesson. + They might misunderstand meanings of words or concepts. + They might lose interest in lessons. + Teachers might assume that a child or young person has SEND.
Children/young people might have difficulty accessing resources in English	
	+ They might understand but need longer to formulate answers. + They might not participate in lessons where quick responses are needed. + They might start to withdraw. + Teachers might think that a child or young person is not interested or has not understood.

Social and emotional needs

Three social and emotional needs are given for this outcome.

Table 12.5 Social and emotional needs

Social and emotional need	Effect
Might be affected by negative attitudes towards their culture, language, ethnicity and religion	Children or young people might: + develop a negative self-concept + not participate in lessons + lose motivation to learn English.
Might feel isolated from their peers	Children or young people might: + not participate in lessons + show unwanted behaviours, e.g. frustration + refuse to attend school or have high rates of absenteeism.
Might not have support available at home to develop EAL	Children or young people might not be able to complete homework that requires English.

Now test yourself   TESTED ●

10 Identify two communication needs that a child or young person might have.

11 Explain how the communication needs of a child or young person might affect their progress in education.

12 Give an example of how an emotional/social need might impact a child's or young person's progress in education.

Exam-style question

4 Using examples, evaluate the impact of social and emotional needs on a child's or young person's progress. [6]

12.5 How practitioners can use a range of strategies to support children/young people being taught EAL

Exam tip

Make sure that you revise this outcome thoroughly. It is likely that you will need to show your knowledge of strategies to support EAL in the assessment for this qualification.

Check your understanding and progress at **www.hoddereducation.co.uk/myrevisionnotes**

Table 12.6 includes ten strategies that practitioners can use, with examples.

Table 12.6 Strategies to support children/young people being taught EAL

Strategy	Explanation	Examples
Using EAL specialist support	Important if a child or young person is having difficulties acquiring English. Might be needed to assess progress in a child's or young person's own language. Advice might be needed to understand a child's or young person's needs.	+ Use of bilingual teaching assistants + Seeking the advice of local EAL team + Using assessments devised by local EAL team
Encouraging peer and group support	Friendships and support of peers can promote positive self-concept.	+ Paired reading + Buddying systems at break time + Encouraging a culture of mutual support
Making the verbal curriculum more visual	Helps children and young people understand more of what is being taught. Makes lessons and activities more interesting. Can help children and young people learn vocabulary.	+ Visual timetables + Using props + Finding images to help explain a concept
Providing opportunities to talk before writing	Discussion of a topic can introduce children and young people to vocabulary that will be needed in writing. Can help children and young people to structure their thoughts and so aid fluent writing.	+ Talking about winter and focusing on words that are associated with winter weather
Using drama and role play	Can introduce new vocabulary. Can help to build confidence. Allows for self-expression and creativity. Can encourage collaboration with others.	+ Home corner play for younger children + Activities that encourage young people to re-enact a scene from a play or to create one
Scaffolding learning	Can help tasks become accessible for children and young people. Can help build children's and young people's proficiency in English as support is structured to meet their current level.	+ Identify which parts of a lesson or activity might be difficult for a child or young person; break down task and support them through it
Creating language-rich environments	Provides opportunities for children and young people to hear language and learn vocabulary in context. Can give children and young people the confidence to talk.	+ Labels on items in the environment + Furniture arranged in ways that promote conversations + Interesting artefacts to provoke comments + Attractive books, posters and images
Providing bilingual resources	Can support the home language alongside English. Can help children and young people to understand equivalent concepts and learn vocabulary in English.	+ Books + Media such as films or programmes with subtitles
Working in partnership with parents/carers	Important in sharing information and understanding the linguistic and cultural background of a child or young person. Can help identify difficulties with the home language. Important in recognising when there may be social and emotional difficulties. Can help parents understand the routines and practices in the setting to promote conversations at home.	+ Formal meetings with parents, aided by an interpreter, if needed + Informal meetings + Film clips that show daily routines in the setting, to show to parents/carers →

Strategy	Explanation	Examples
Celebrating an individual's culture	Promotes positive self-concept. Helps peers and others in the setting learn more about an individual's home culture. Link between feeling valued and progress in education.	+ Bringing in music and artefacts that reflect the cultural identity of a child or young person + Playing games that are used in the culture + Encouraging child or young person to talk about their culture
Positive outcomes of multi-lingualism	Promotes stronger self-identity. Helps gain greater connections to family members. Provides cognitive benefits, as using more than one language requires more flexible thinking.	+ All adults in the educational setting need to promote a positive attitude towards different languages. + Recognition that EAL is not the same category as SEND.

Making links

Element 5, Section 5.1, discusses the advantages of working with parents, families and carers. List three advantages of working with parents.

Revision activity

Write down reasons why each of the following strategies might be beneficial:
+ making the verbal curriculum more visual
+ providing opportunities to talk before writing
+ using drama and role play
+ creating language-rich environments
+ working in partnership with parents/carers.

Now test yourself

TESTED

13 Explain why using visual resources and props might support a child or young person learning EAL.

14 How might the use of peer support help a child or young person who is learning EAL?

15 Why is it important that a child's or young person's culture is celebrated?

Exam tip

Make sure that your answer reflects that individual children and young people will have varying needs. A combination of strategies might be needed.

Typical mistake

Make sure that your example of how to support a child or young person is age-appropriate. For example, don't suggest that a 14-year-old could be given a book that was designed for a 4-year-old.

Exam-style questions

5 Evaluate the importance of using a range of strategies to support a five-year-old child who is learning English as an additional language. [6]

6 Gulhan is five years old. She has been in school for one term. She has not made any friends and her parents say that she has always been a shy child who enjoys her own company. She began at nursery, but did not settle and so stopped going.

When asked about her language at home, Gulhan's parents say that she is not talking as well as they had hoped. In class, Gulhan seems anxious. She does not say anything and does not seem to have learnt the routine of the school day. The school has started to use a visual timetable, and she now recognises when it is lunchtime and also home time. Her teacher has observed that her play is limited and that she does not make eye contact or attempt to play with the other children.

A Identify Gulhan's stage of English acquisition. [1]

B Discuss the factors affecting Gulhan's acquisition of language. [6]

C Assess various ways in which adults might support Gulhan's development. [6]

Check your understanding and progress at **www.hoddereducation.co.uk/myrevisionnotes**

Glossary

AAC (augmentative and alternative communication) This term is used to cover all types of communication methods that enhance or replace speech, such as sign language or technical devices.

Accountable Required to justify actions or decisions.

Anaemia A health condition in which there are not enough red blood cells in the body, meaning the body might not receive enough oxygen.

Asocial stage Baby is neither sociable nor unsociable.

Attachment An emotional bond.

Benchmark A point of reference for checking standards.

Bilingualism The ability to use more than one language.

Blended learning A style of teaching that uses a blend of online and face-to-face teaching.

Continuing professional development (CPD) Ongoing professional training and development.

Core subjects English, maths and science.

DBS check The DBS (Disclosure and Barring Service – formerly CRB) check is a legal requirement for those working with children and young people. It applies to the health and social care sectors and those working in education and early years.

Developmental delay A delay in one or more areas of a child's or young person's development.

Differentiate To tailor instructions and set work according to the needs/level of children and young people.

Disclosure Being told about something; in this situation a disclosure of grooming or abuse.

Discrimination Different (usually unfair) treatment of a group of people due to prejudice.

Disengaged Where a child or young person is not motivated to learn.

Disorganised-disoriented Term used when child's behaviour during separation cannot be categorised.

Diversity The existence of differences between individuals.

DSL (Designated Safeguarding Lead) Person in a school or setting who is responsible for all safeguarding issues.

Dyscalculia A learning difficulty which mainly affects a person's ability to use numbers.

Dyslexia A learning difficulty which mainly affects a person's reading and writing skills.

EAL English as an additional language.

Early Learning Goals Age-appropriate expectations in each area of development at the end of the EYFS.

Early production Being able to say or repeat some words.

Education, Health and Care Plan (EHCP) A document which sets out the provision needed for a child or young person who has SEND.

Enabling language Using language which makes the individual feel that they are able to do something.

Equality Being equal in terms of status, rights and opportunities.

Experiential Learning from experience.

EYFS Early Years Foundation Stage.

EYFS Profile Assessment carried out in school at the end of the Reception year.

Fluency Being able to understand and use a language quickly and easily.

Formative feedback This provides information that will help a child or young person to make progress.

Further education colleges These include general FE and tertiary colleges, sixth form colleges and specialist colleges, as well as adult education provision.

Holistic Looking at all the interconnecting parts of something as a whole, rather than individually.

Impulse control The ability to reflect rather than act in the moment.

Inclusion The process of identifying, understanding and breaking down barriers to participation and belonging.

Innate Something that occurs naturally.

Insecure ambivalent Before and after separation, the child is clingy and fearful, and shows difficult behaviours.

Insecure avoidant Before and during separation, little exploration. During separation, the baby does not react when the parent leaves or returns.

Local safeguarding partnerships Statutory local organisations set up to promote the safeguarding and welfare of children and young people, and to co-ordinate local healthcare, education and local authority providers.

Looked after child (LAC) A child who has been in the care of their local authority for more than 24 hours.

Neurodevelopmental Relating to the development of the central nervous system, for example, in the case of autistic spectrum conditions.

Neurological Relating to or affecting the brain and nervous system.

Ofsted A government department which has responsibility for inspecting services providing education and skills, including those who care for babies, children and young people.

Paired reading Where a child and an adult or a more fluent child reader share a book together.

Parallel play Playing next to another child but not with them.

Primary disability The main physical or mental impairment that has a negative effect on a person's ability to carry out normal activities. The individual may have other impairments resulting from or apart from this.

Pupil premium Money given by the government to schools to raise the attainment of disadvantaged pupils.

Ratify To vote on a written document to accept it as official.

RBA (Reception Baseline Assessment) Assessment that is carried out at the start of a child's Reception year in school.

Reasonable adjustment A change which is made to reduce the disadvantage which a person has due to their disability.

Regulation A set of rules or laws to control and protect the way in which something is done.

Safeguarding Action taken to promote the welfare of children and protect them from harm.

Sanction The stated consequence for a child or young person of showing unwanted behaviour.

School-readiness strategies The skills children need to cope with the start of school.

Secure attachment Before separation, the child explores the environment and interacts with strangers. After separation, the child is distressed but soon calms down when mother appears.

Selective education Education in which the students have been admitted through a selection process such as a test.

Self-regulation Our ability to control our own emotions, thoughts and behaviour, adjust to changing situations and cope with unexpected stress.

SEND (or SEN) 'A child or young person has SEN if they have a learning difficulty or disability which calls for special educational provision to be made for him or her' (SEND Code of Practice 2015).

Sensory processing The way in which an individual receives and processes information through the senses.

Social mobility Movement of individuals or groups between different social classes or levels.

Social norms Behaviour shown and expected by others in any given situation.

Socio-economic circumstances The income and education level of a household.

Statutory Something that is required by law.

Synthetic phonics A system of teaching reading and writing which involves breaking down the sounds in words to their smallest components, e.g. s-t-i-ck-er.

Tertiary colleges Institutions which provide general and vocational FE for students aged 16–19. They are distinct from general FE colleges as they cater for a specific age group and offer a less extensive and varied curriculum.

Transition An expected or unexpected change in a child's or young person's life which can affect their behaviour or development. This includes, for example, moving to secondary school, parents divorcing or the family moving house.

Vulnerable adult A person over 18 who needs additional care due to a physical or mental disability or illness.

Whistleblowing Reporting a co-worker for something that is wrong and that affects others.

Index

Check your understanding and progress at **www.hoddereducation.co.uk/myrevisionnotes**

Check your understanding and progress at **www.hoddereducation.co.uk/myrevisionnotes**